# Insights You Need from Harvard Business Review

**Business is changing. Will you adapt or be left behind?**

Get up to speed and deepen your understanding of the topics that are shaping your company's future with the **Insights You Need from Harvard Business Review series**. Featuring HBR's smartest thinking on fast-moving issues—blockchain, cybersecurity, AI, and more—each book provides the foundational introduction and practical case studies your organization needs to compete today and collects the best research, interviews, and analysis to get it ready for tomorrow.

You can't afford to ignore how these issues will transform the landscape of business and society. The Insights You Need series will help you grasp these critical ideas—and prepare you and your company for the future.

## Books in the series includes:

*Agile*

*Artificial Intelligence*

*Blockchain*

*Climate Change*

*Coronavirus: Leadership and Recovery*

*Customer Data and Privacy*

*Cybersecurity*

*Monopolies and Tech Giants*

*Strategic Analytics*

*The Year in Tech, 2021*

Insights You Need from
**Harvard Business Review**

# CORONAVIRUS: LEADERSHIP AND RECOVERY

Harvard Business Review Press
Boston, Massachusetts

Copyright 2020 Harvard Business School Publishing Corporation
All rights reserved
Printed in the United States of America

10 9 8 7 6 5 4 3 2 1

The web addresses referenced in this book were live and correct at the time of the book's publication but may be subject to change.

Cataloging-in-Publication data is forthcoming.

ISBN: 978-1-64782-049-7
eISBN: 978-1-64782-050-3

The paper used in this publication meets the requirements of the American National Standard for Permanence of Paper for Publications and Documents in Libraries and Archives Z39.48-1992

# Contents

Section 2

# Managing Your Workforce

Section 3

# Managing Yourself

Section 4
## Seeing Beyond the Crisis

Contents

# Introduction

# BROADENING YOUR PERSPECTIVE ON CRISIS LEADERSHIP

by Martin Reeves

In the midst of the Covid-19 pandemic, the topic of crisis management is at the forefront in business conversations worldwide. This concentration on surviving the immediate crisis is understandable and useful in the short term—it enables us to focus on the immediate, high-stakes issues we are all facing. But with constant urgency and stress comes a narrowing of perspectives and time horizons. This inhibits deeper and broader reflection, which is necessary in responding effectively to the crisis, rebounding from it, and reinventing our businesses after it passes. A return to long-term and broader thinking won't happen by default. One of the key roles for leaders, now that the initial shock is behind us, is to legitimize and foster a rebroadening of perspectives.

In my role as Chairman of the BCG Henderson Institute, I've interacted with hundreds of companies in client roundtables over the past few weeks, and it has struck me that many companies are still stuck in *reacting* to the immediate crisis. Reaction is only the first stage of a multistage game. The urge to minimize damage will never, for example, result in designing creative strategies to address new needs and shape the emergence of new market segments. To balance crisis management with thinking holistically about the crisis and its aftermath, leaders need to reframe their thinking and action appropriately as each phase unfolds.

A few years ago, I coauthored a book titled *Your Strategy Needs a Strategy*, which proposed that different situations call not only for different strategies but for different *approaches* to strategy and problem solving. Specifically, we proposed a *strategy palette*, comprising five distinct styles of problem solving: classical (plan driven), adaptive (iterative experimentation and adjustment), shaping (coevolution and collaboration), visionary (creative), and renewal (turnaround). Each style requires adopting the right model, tools, metrics, behaviors, and leadership styles to effectively respond to the situation at hand.

In the language of the strategy palette, companies facing Covid-19 need to create *temporal ambidexterity*: the ability to switch and apply different problem-solving styles over time. First, we need to react urgently and pragmatically to the crisis, using a *renewal* approach. But after this reactionary phase we need to implement planned measures to manage cash burn in the now inevitable economic downturn, using a *classical* style. As the disease and the economic aftermath develop unpredictably, we need to learn rapidly about the latest developments and flex our tactics accordingly, using an *adaptive* style. Every crisis contains opportunity, and once the acute phase of the disease is controlled and the economic aftermath managed, we will need to think about capturing opportunities in the new post-Covid reality, using *visionary* and *shaping* styles.

This broadening of how we think about and manage the crisis (and the opportunity) will need to take place at multiple levels: the individual, the company, the industry, the country, and the globe. The unprecedented nature of this "Great Pause" means that few companies and managers will have experienced such a rapid succession of problem-solving styles. It is therefore very encouraging to see *HBR* mobilizing with extraordinary speed to help leaders and managers by promptly compiling this book of broader perspectives on managing the crisis, the recovery, and the post-Covid era. This collection will help leaders who are learning on the fly understand what moves they need to make to ensure that their enterprises not only endure but flourish through the major discontinuity we are living through.

The first section, "Leading Your Business," covers the key leadership behaviors needed in a crisis. It takes a high-level view of the legal risks around Covid-19 that no company must overlook, then explores how we can take inspiration from history's greatest leaders in the most challenging moments.

Next, the "Managing Your Workforce" section acknowledges that while the initial shock of remote work has worn off for many, bolstering a culture of innovation, keeping remote workers engaged, and having difficult conversations (including, unfortunately, informing employees about layoffs) remain challenging. It looks at how the best retailers are keeping their employees safe and gives guidance on actions to take when one of your employees tests positive for Covid-19.

The "Managing Yourself" section addresses how we can deal individually with a society-wide emergency. It has never been clearer that work life, personal life, physical health, and mental health are more closely intertwined than many businesses previously acknowledged. These chapters address important topics like how to avoid burnout and how to manage stress in dire times, and they help us understand how to find meaning in our collective grief.

The final section, "Seeing Beyond the Crisis," brings forward the kind of thinking that will be needed to adopt the visionary and shaping strategies to revitalize and reinvent your business for eventual recovery. It helps readers consider how the economic recovery from coronavirus might unfold over time, looks closely at how you can ensure that your customer relationships outlast the pandemic, and speculates on how the landscape of labor laws and practices may be permanently reoriented. Finally, it encourages businesses to cultivate the culture of imagination necessary to build a successful future.

This is a moment when great leaders and businesses will rise to the occasion. As Nancy Koehn shows in her contribution to this collection, leadership is often forged in crises. Leaders become "real" in difficult times, not only when they steel people with resolve and purpose but also when they inspire people to experiment and learn through the crisis, turning adversity into opportunity.

# Section 1

# LEADING YOUR BUSINESS

# FOUR BEHAVIORS THAT HELP LEADERS MANAGE A CRISIS

by Chris Nichols, Shoma Chatterjee Hayden, and Chris Trendler

The roles and responsibilities of business leaders have dramatically changed in the past few weeks. Before Covid-19, CEOs and other executives in high-growth companies were focused on fostering innovation, driving revenue, and gaining market share. Today, many of those same leaders must make rapid decisions about controlling costs and maintaining liquidity. They may encounter unforeseen roadblocks—supply chain issues, team shortages, and operational challenges—that drastically alter the scope of their roles and priorities. All the while, they and their teams are navigating health and safety concerns, working remotely, and supporting their families through the pandemic.

This is not an easy transition. Those in charge will be tested in areas where they have not fully developed their leadership muscles, and the learning curve will be steep. They will need coaching from their own bosses and others.

Having conducted more than 21,000 leadership assessments among C-suite executives, our research team at ghSMART has learned that to move forward in a crisis, leaders need to cultivate four behaviors in themselves and their teams. They must decide with speed over precision, adapt boldly, deliver reliably, and engage for impact. The tactics below can guide you as you coach your leaders in these key behaviors.

# Behavior 1: Decide with Speed over Precision

The situation is changing by the day—even by the hour. The best leaders quickly process available information, rapidly determine what matters most, and make decisions with conviction. During a crisis, cognitive overload looms; information is incomplete, interests and priorities may clash, and emotions and anxieties run high.

Analysis paralysis can easily result, exacerbated by the natural tendency of matrixed organizations to build consensus. Leaders must break through the inertia to keep the organization trained on business continuity today while increasing the odds of mid- to long-term success by focusing on the few things that matter most. A simple, scalable framework for rapid decision making is critical. You and your leaders should:

- Define priorities. Identify and communicate the three to five most important ones. Early in the crisis, those might include employee safety and care, financial liquidity, customer care, and operational continuity. Document the issues identified, ensure that leadership is fully aligned with them, and make course corrections as events unfold.

- Make smart trade-offs. What conflicts might arise among the priorities you have outlined? Between the urgent and the important? Between survival today and success tomorrow? Instead of thinking about all possibilities, the best leaders use their priorities as a scoring mechanism to force trade-offs.

- Name the decision makers. In your central command "war room," establish who owns what. Empower the front line to make decisions where possible, and clearly state what needs to be escalated, by when, and to whom. Your default should be to push decisions downward, not up.

- Embrace action, and don't punish mistakes. Missteps will happen, but our research indicates that failing to act is much worse.

## Behavior 2: Adapt Boldly

Strong leaders get ahead of changing circumstances. They seek input and information from diverse sources, are not afraid to admit what they don't know, and bring in outside expertise when needed.

You and your leaders should:

- Decide what not to do. Put a hold on large initiatives and expenses, and ruthlessly prioritize. Publicize your "what not to do" choices.

- Throw out yesterday's playbook. The actions that previously drove results may no longer be relevant. The best leaders adjust quickly and develop new plans of attack.

- Strengthen (or build) direct connections to the front line. In triage situations, it's crucial to have an accurate, current picture of what is happening on the ground. Whether running a supply chain, leading a waste management company, or overseeing a pharmaceutical company, leaders must get situational assessments early and often. One way is to create a network of local leaders and influencers who can speak with deep knowledge about the impact of the crisis and the sentiments of customers, suppliers, employees, and other stakeholders. Technology can bring the parties together; think internal wikis that capture issues, solutions, innovations, and best practices. Effective leaders extend their antennae across all the ecosystems in which they operate.

## Behavior 3: Deliver Reliably

The best leaders take personal ownership in a crisis, even though many challenges and factors lie outside their control. They align team focus, establish new metrics to monitor performance, and create a culture of accountability.

You and your leaders should:

- Stay alert to and aligned on a daily dashboard of priorities. Leaders should succinctly document their top five priorities (on half a page or less) and ensure that those above them are in accord. Review performance against those items frequently—if not daily, perhaps weekly—and make sure that leaders share this information with direct reports. Review and update your "hit list" at the end of each day or week.

- Set key performance indicators and other metrics to measure performance. Choose three to five metrics that matter most for the week, and have leaders regularly report back on each.

- Keep mind and body in fighting shape. To reliably deliver, leaders must maintain their equanimity even when others are losing their heads. Establish a routine of self-care: a healthy diet, exercise, meditation, or whatever works best for you. Stock up on energy, emotional reserves, and coping mechanisms.

## Behavior 4: Engage for Impact

In times of crisis, no job is more important than taking care of your team. Effective leaders are understanding of their team's circumstances and distractions, but they find ways to engage and motivate, clearly and thoroughly communicating important new goals and information. This point deserves extra attention, because although the Covid-19 pandemic is, of course, a health crisis, it has sparked a financial crisis as well. Your leaders need to reiterate new priorities frequently to ensure continued alignment in this time of constant and stressful change.

You and your leaders should:

- Connect with individual team members. Reach out daily for a "pulse check" with at least five; block out time on the calendar to do this. Relate on a personal level first, and then focus on work. One leader we know conducts thirty-minute "wind down" sessions with direct reports each Friday afternoon via Zoom. People share their states of mind along with the week's highlights and low points.

- Dig deep to engage your teams. When communication breaks down and leaders act without team input, as can more easily happen when work is remote, they get subpar results.

- Ask for help as needed. The best leaders know they can't do everything themselves. Identify team structures and assign individuals to support key efforts.

- Ensure a focus on both customers and employees. To support customers: Reach out, but first do no harm. Track and document intel across your customer base. To strengthen relationships and build trust, keep the focus off yourself, and explore how you can truly help your customers—for example, by proposing payment schedules to ease their liquidity crunch or offering pro bono or in-kind provision of services. To support employees: Lead with empathy and a focus on safety and health. Compassion goes a long way during turbulent times. Find ways to lend material aid to frontline employees who cannot work remotely, such as first responders, couriers, and trash collectors.

- Collect and amplify positive messages about things like successes, acts of kindness, and obstacles that have been overcome. Many companies are tied to a noble purpose, such as saving lives, manufacturing medical equipment, helping markets function more efficiently, or providing joy. Whatever your purpose, celebrate your daily (often unsung) heroes. Simply staying productive in these times is heroic.

## Training Your Team for Crisis Leadership

As a leader of leaders, you are navigating new and ever-changing priorities with limited time to react. Some small investments in support and coaching can go a long way toward boosting your leaders' effectiveness.

Moments of crisis reveal a great deal about the leaders below you. Once the immediate fire is under control and you have a moment to catch your breath, think about who rose to the occasion, who struggled, and why. Consider how roles will change in the postcrisis world and whether your key executives are positioned for success. Last and most important, ask yourself whom you want at the table both in the current crisis and in the longed-for tomorrow when we emerge to a new normal.

TAKEAWAYS

Covid-19 is challenging leaders in areas where they have not yet tested their leadership muscles. Many are experiencing a drastically altered scope of their roles and priorities and will need coaching as they learn new skills on the fly.

✓ Employees thrust into leadership during a crisis need to be coached in four behaviors to be most effective in their roles: They must decide with speed over precision; adapt to changing circumstances boldly; reliably deliver despite environmental factors; and engage deeply with their teams.

✓ Remember that moments of crisis can tell you a great deal about those under you. Identify who rose to the occasion, who struggled, and why. Ask yourself whom you want at the table both during the crisis and after.

*Adapted from "4 Behaviors That Help Leaders Manage a Crisis" on hbr.org, April 2, 2020 (product #H05IAR).*

# 2

# WHAT ARE COMPANIES' LEGAL OBLIGATIONS AROUND CORONAVIRUS?

by Peter Susser and Tahl Tyson

W ith the rapid global spread of coronavirus, companies should focus first on employee safety. And as they're reviewing their strategies, policies, and procedures, many leaders are specifically wondering about their legal risk. Not having adequate communicable-illness policies and response plans could expose them to a laundry list of HR-related legal concerns.

Most countries have laws designed to protect employees from physical harm at work. In the United States, employees are protected under the Occupational Safety and Health Act, so if an employee becomes infected at work, in some circumstances the employer may face penalties. Unprepared employers may be exposed to lawsuits related to workers' compensation, invasion of privacy, discrimination, unfair labor practices, and negligence.

The good news is that with careful attention to employee safety and legal preparedness, employers can minimize employees' risk of infection and their own legal risks. Following are eight steps companies should take to these ends. The value of these efforts, of course, is relevant to any life-threatening infectious disease, not just coronavirus.

## Stay Informed

Start by identifying authoritative sources of public health guidance on the epidemic, and stay up to date on officially recommended and mandated actions in the applicable jurisdictions. These sources include the Centers for Disease Control and Prevention, the World Health

Organization, the European Center for Disease Prevention and Control, and country-specific guidance from public health organizations.

This official guidance should serve as the foundation for organizational decisions about health- and legal-risk mitigation. Being able to demonstrate corporate policy alignment with official recommendations can be an important legal safeguard in cases where the company's infection-control efforts are challenged.

## Intensify Communications and Hygiene

For legal and practical reasons, companies need to be able to show that they have given employees accurate information about ways to prevent the spread of infection—and that they have provided people with the means to act on that information. Thus, organizations should educate employees, in advance of any workplace infection, about modes of transmission and symptoms by sharing specific public health guidelines and, more broadly, directing staff to the official sources of information on which the organization will rely.

In addition, employers must implement measures to reduce the risk of workplace transmission. For example, public health guidance for reducing transmission includes ensuring that employees have easy access to handwashing facilities and/or hand sanitizers and that public surfaces such as counters, doorknobs, and elevator buttons are regularly disinfected. Employers may also consider changes to reduce overcrowding, such as facilitating remote work, shift work, and perhaps changes to physical layout. Such measures may help protect workers from infection and help protect organizations from liability.

Employers should also instruct staff to inform management if they have been exposed to the virus or show symptoms of infection, or if they, or a member of their household, have particular vulnerabilities such as a weakened immune system that may require enhanced protections from infection. Further, staff with symptoms of infection should be sent home or instructed to stay home, and visitors who have been exposed or who have symptoms should be excluded from the workplace. Failure to provide this guidance can potentially expose a company to liability should employees become infected in the workplace and it can be shown that management had not communicated about this policy. (Although disability discrimination laws protect employees with covered health conditions, limitations can generally be imposed if there's a direct threat to the health or safety of others.)

## Consider Restrictions on Returning to Work

While employers risk discrimination claims if they base decisions to restrict employees from work on grounds of race or national origin, they can impose reasonable, fact-based restrictions if there is a direct threat to the health or safety of others. An employer can judge, by applying official guidelines or with input from a medical consultant, whether and when an employee who has been ill or who has potentially been exposed can safely return to work. Written policies should be explicit about when employees with potentially transmissible conditions will and will not be allowed back, and relevant communications should be documented.

## Be Mindful of an Employer's Duty of Care

Most countries have laws designed to protect employees from physical harm at work. For multinational employers and those with mobile employees, it is important to identify the applicable country laws (which may be more than those of a single jurisdiction in some cases), as one size will not fit all.

In the United States, employees are protected under the Occupational Safety and Health Act (OSH Act). Section 5(a)(1) of the OSH Act is the general duty clause, which requires employers to provide their employees with a workplace "free from recognized hazards . . . likely to cause death or serious physical harm." The federal Occupational Safety and Health Administration (OSHA) can cite employers for violating the general duty clause if there is a recognized hazard and they do not take reasonable steps to prevent or abate the hazard. However, OSHA citations can only be based on standards, regulations, or the general duty clause.

State-mandated workers' compensation programs, and a separate program for federal workers, provide benefits to eligible employees who suffer job-related injuries and illnesses (these vary state by state). As a rule, when the harm arises out of and in the course of employment, employees are limited to the prescribed workers' compensation benefits and cannot recover damages for pain and suffering or mental anguish. Some states allow additional awards—beyond normal workers' compensation awards—when injury results from an employer's "willful" or "intentional" act, which might include failure to provide appropriate protections.

Businesses also have to consider liability to third parties, such as customers, which may not be so limited. For example, a restaurant employee infected on the job will only be entitled to workers' compensation, but theoretically the patrons they may infect could seek greater damages.

## Evaluate Leave and Pay

Employers should analyze their legal obligations to provide employees with leave in the event of sickness or disability and evaluate whether their policies need to be adjusted in the current circumstances. In the United States, the Family and Medical Leave Act (FMLA), the Americans with Disabilities Act (ADA), and state laws will apply, as well as any contract and policy language. Exclusions from insurance policies should be identified—for example, many travel insurance policies exclude pandemics.

Drawing on this analysis, companies should consider under which circumstances they would want to extend or expand benefits and protections, and they should evaluate their level of income protection for employees on leave, perhaps adjusting benefits plans for employees who exceed their sick-day allotment in order to support sick employees who must stay home.

It is important to look beyond the immediate legal requirements to the broader business and legal implications.

For example, a business may not be legally required to pay an employee during a period it bars him or her from the workplace because that individual was on personal travel to a place where transmission was occurring. However, choosing not to do so makes it more likely that they return to work prematurely, thereby infecting other staff, risking business continuity, incurring legal liability from third parties such as customers, and contributing to an increase in infections.

## Alleviate Stress and Anxiety

Stress and anxiety related to coronavirus infection could also become a legal concern. The legal standards will vary by jurisdiction. For example, employers in the United Kingdom have a duty to assess the risk of stress-related, ill health arising from work activities, and they are required to take reasonable measures to control such risks. In some cases, this may mean taking steps beyond the minimum if doing so is not unduly burdensome to the employer and mitigates the psychological burden on the employee. For example, rather than terminating an employee for refusing to come to the office due to fear of contagion, even though all officially recommended precautions have been taken, an employer might be more flexible in allowing time off or remote working arrangements. Such steps can help U.K. employers avoid claims of unfair dismissal.

Employers should be aware that a mental health condition such as germophobia may be protected as a disability under laws such as ADA, which would necessitate employers taking a modified approach pursuant to reasonable accommodation requirements.

## Protect Privacy

Employers should understand which personal health data an employee might be obligated to disclose if he or she becomes infected or is at high risk for infection—likely, anything that could interfere with the employee's ability to perform the essential functions of the job, or that could increase the risk to coworkers or third parties through workplace contact. Failure to understand the legal obligations in relation to such data could expose the company to breach of privacy claims.

Fortunately, even rigorous privacy rules allow employers to disclose employees' protected health information to authorities for public health purposes. That said, all such data must be handled within the organization's data privacy protection framework, and if such data is being transmitted from the European Union to the United States, care should be taken to do so in compliance with the General Data Protection Regulation (GDPR).

## Plan for a Worst-Case Scenario

Contingency planning may include, for example, temporary succession planning for key decision makers and understanding and preparing in advance for the legal requirements in cases of furloughs and layoffs. Many jurisdictions require more formal procedures and notifications for layoffs above a certain number of employees. A failure to comply can have severe penalties for employers and even personal liability in some cases for their leadership. Planning ahead in order to stay compliant is an important part of an organization's resilience program.

TAKEAWAYS

Having inadequate communicable-illness policies and response plans related to coronavirus could expose your company to a number of HR-related legal concerns, including those related to workers' compensation, invasion of privacy, discrimination, unfair labor practice, and negligence lawsuits. Careful attention to employee safety and legal preparedness can minimize employees' risk of infection and an employer's legal risks. Your company should take eight steps:

✓ Stay informed

✓ Intensify communications and hygiene

✓ Consider restrictions on returning to work

✓ Be mindful of an employer's duty of care

✓ Evaluate leave and pay

✓ Alleviate stress and anxiety

✓ Protect privacy

✓ Plan for a worst-case scenario

*Adapted from "What Are Companies' Legal Obligations Around Coronavirus?" on hbr.org, March 4, 2020 (product #H05GMA).*

# 3

# REAL LEADERS ARE FORGED IN CRISIS

by Nancy Koehn

W e are living through a global health crisis with no modern-day precedent. What governments, corporations, hospitals, schools, and other organizations need now, more than ever, are what the writer David Foster Wallace called "real leaders"—people who "help us overcome the limitations of our own individual laziness and selfishness and weakness and fear and get us to do better, harder things than we can get ourselves to do on our own."

I have studied courageous crisis leaders for two decades, and through this work I know that real leaders are not born; the ability to help others triumph over adversity is not written into their genetic code. They are, instead, made. They are forged in crisis. Leaders become "real" when they practice a few key behaviors that gird and inspire people through difficult times. As Covid-19 tears its way through country after country, town after town, neighborhood after neighborhood, here's what we can learn from how some of history's iconic leaders acted in the face of great uncertainty, real danger, and collective fear.

## Acknowledge People's Fears, Then Encourage Resolve

Most of us know the famous lines of U.S. president Franklin Delano Roosevelt's 1933 inaugural address in the midst of the Great Depression: "The only thing we have to fear is . . . fear itself." He followed that by pointing to the nation's strengths in meeting the crisis: "This is no unsolvable problem if we face it wisely and courageously. There are many ways in which it can be helped, but it can never be helped merely by talking about it. We must act and act quickly."

Less than a decade later, as the United Kingdom stared down the Nazi onslaught in the Second World War, Prime

Minister Winston Churchill encouraged his people to keep the faith: "We shall not fail or falter; we shall not weaken or tire. Neither the sudden shock of battle, nor the long-drawn trials of vigilance and exertion will wear us down. Give us the tools, and we will finish the job."

In the business world, consider examples like Katharine Graham, leader of the *Washington Post* in 1971, who moved through her own fears by vowing that the free press would not cave to government demands to stop publication of the Pentagon Papers. She then helped her editors and journalists do the same, as the newspaper began printing a series of revelatory articles and excerpts about U.S. involvement in Vietnam. Or think about Ed Stack, CEO of Dick's Sporting Goods, who, when confronted with the extraordinary increase in school shootings in the United States, persuaded his board and management team to risk the ire of gun rights' advocates and a significant decline in revenue by discontinuing the sale of firearms at its namesake stores.

Your job as a leader today is to provide both brutal honesty—a clear accounting of the challenges your locality, company, nonprofit, or team faces—and credible hope that collectively you and your people have the resources needed to meet the threats you face each day: determination, solidarity, strength, shared purpose, humanity, kindness, and resilience. Recognize that most of your employees are anxious about their health, their finances, and, in many cases, their jobs. Explain that you understand how scary things feel, but that you can work together to weather this storm.

If you're looking for in-the-moment role models, turn to Governor Andrew Cuomo of New York or Governor Gretchen Whitmer of Michigan, both of whom are offering de facto master classes in crisis leadership: explaining the gravity of the situations their states are facing, outlining the resources being deployed to battle the coronavirus, and calling their constituents to act from their stronger, more compassionate selves.

Inspire your followers with the words of the Reverend William Sloane Coffin: "Courage is a crucial virtue. Will we be scared to death, or scared to life?"

## Give People a Role and a Purpose

Real leaders charge individuals to act in service of the broader community. They give people jobs to do.

During the U.S. Civil War, for example, President Abraham Lincoln exhorted and ordered men of the Northern states to fight; as the civil rights movement gathered momentum in the late 1950s and early 1960s, the Reverend Martin Luther King Jr. asked his followers to sit in, march, and otherwise protest racial discrimination. In his first inaugural address, FDR told his countrymen to keep their money in the banks as an important way of averting a banking crisis; later, his wife, First Lady Eleanor Roosevelt, encouraged American women to work in the nation's factories, while their fathers, brothers, husbands, and sons went to battle in the Second World War.

On a smaller scale, we can look to Antarctic explorer Ernest Shackleton's leadership. When, in 1915, his expedition ship the *Endurance* became stuck in the ice and he realized that he and his crew would have to wait out the brutal winter on a floating iceberg, he insisted that each man maintain his ordinary duties: sailors swabbed decks, scientists collected specimens, others were assigned to hunt for meat. He knew that daily routines and tasks, including manual labor, would help establish order and thus ground his men in an uncertain time that was filled with danger.

In the current crisis, leaders must act in a similar fashion, giving their followers direction and reminding them why their work matters. In organizations providing essential services—such as government agencies, hospitals, pharmacies, grocery stores, food and health-care-equipment manufacturing plants, news outlets, scientific labs, non-profits serving the poor, and many others—this raison d'etre will be immediately apparent. But it's still vitally important to emphasize the key role that each person plays. In other businesses, the new mission can be as simple as helping all stakeholders navigate this crisis as effectively as possible. For us at Harvard Business School and *HBR*, that means teaching and publishing lessons like these. At a Nebraska truck stop, which Karen Gettert Shoemaker's family has run for years, she and others are focused on keeping the truckers who provide essential goods moving across the country, offering them a welcoming pit stop on their journeys.

When in doubt about what you or your team can do during this pandemic, prioritize helping others—even in the smallest ways. When I was going through a particularly difficult period in my life, I heard a sermon by Peter Gomes, who was then minister at Harvard's Memorial Church, that reminded me of the transformative power of giving. "When in the midst of [outer] turmoil and calamity you seek the inner strength that helps you not only to endure but to overcome, do not look for what you can get," he told his audience. "Look rather for what you have been given, and for what you can give." When we help others, even in the smallest ways, our fear ebbs and our focus sharpens.

## Emphasize Experimentation and Learning

To successfully navigate crisis, strong leaders quickly get comfortable with widespread ambiguity and chaos, recognizing that they do not have a crisis playbook. Instead, they commit themselves and their followers to navigating from point to point through the turbulence, adjusting, improvising, and redirecting as the situation changes and new information emerges. Courageous leaders also understand that they will make mistakes along the way and will have to pivot quickly as this happens, learning as they go.

During his long, dark winter on the *Endurance*, Shackleton constantly responded to changing circumstances. When his ship got stuck, he shifted his mission from exploration to survival. When the ship was no longer habitable, he instructed his men to build a camp on the ice. When he finally got his team to an uninhabited island, where he knew there was no chance of outside rescue, he and a small group of his men sailed one of the three lifeboats eight hundred miles to another island, where he knew he could find help. Four months and three thwarted rescue attempts later, Shackleton finally arrived back at the original island to the rest of his team. They were all alive, and he brought them home.

During the Cuban Missile Crisis in late 1962, President John F. Kennedy demonstrated the same agility: At each juncture of the standoff between the United States and the Soviet Union, he ordered his small team of advisers to work to expand his options rather than committing to and blindly following one course of action.

Emphasize to your followers that you expect everyone—individually and as a group—(to learn their way forward, to experiment with new ways of operating, to expect the occasional failure and quickly pivot to a new tack, to figure out the future together.)In fact, this crisis—including the social-distancing measures it has required and the widespread economic downturn following closely in its wake—presents a powerful opportunity for organizations and teams of all kinds to better understand their strengths and weaknesses, what really engages and motivates their people, and their own reason for being.

## Tend to Energy and Emotion—Yours and Theirs

Crises take a toll on all of us. They are exhausting and can lead to burnout. For those who lose loved ones, they are devastating. Thus, one critical function of leadership during intense turbulence is to keep your finger on the pulse of your people's energy and emotions and respond as needed.

When tending to energy and emotion, you must begin with yourself. As a high-ranking executive commented before the pandemic, "If you as the leader flag, everything flags. Everything else, including your organization's mission, becomes vulnerable." So in these trying times, take good care of yourself physically, emotionally, and spiritually. Know when you are capable of being focused and productive and when you need a break. Eat well; get enough sleep; exercise regularly; spend time outdoors (six feet away from strangers); connect in person with your partner, kids, or animals and virtually with friends and extended family; plan for at least two device-free periods per day (for a minimum of thirty minutes each); and rely on other practices that help you get grounded.

Next, model the behavior you want to see. This means using your body language, words, and actions to signal that we are moving forward with conviction and courage. It means regularly taking the (figurative) temperature of your team—How are they doing? How are they feeling? What do they need?—so that its members begin to do the same for each other. Indicate that you are taking the time to rest and recharge, and encourage your employees to do the same. As New York governor Andrew Cuomo has told the citizens of New York, "Take a walk," and "Call

Mom." Another quick way to boost morale is by cultivating gratitude. Ask your people to list three things each day for which they feel grateful. And circle back regularly to the three points listed above: demonstrate resolve, emphasize role and mission, and focus on the opportunity for learning.

Last week, one of my dearest friends died from Covid-19. For more than eleven years, he and his wife, who is now hospitalized for the disease, have been my guardian angels—moving into my home to nurse me when I had chemotherapy infusions for cancer in 2009, checking in on me when things went wrong, and spending holidays with me. They have both been bright, shining lights in my life, encouraging me to push through the hard times and raising my spirits. The grief I feel in the wake of Steven's passing is searing. Yet even as I weep for him and all he meant to the world and me, I still hear him saying, "You are stronger than you know, Nancy. You can do this." That is what all leaders must communicate to their followers right now.

We—all of us—will be remembered for how we manage ourselves and others through this crisis. How will you, your team, your organization, our society connect, persevere, and progress? How will we emerge from this experience collectively stronger?

**TAKEAWAYS**

Leaders become "real" leaders when they practice a few key behaviors that gird and inspire people through difficult times. As Covid-19 tears its way through country after country, town after town, neighborhood after neighborhood, we can learn from how some of history's iconic leaders—Lincoln, Churchill, Kennedy, FDR, Katharine Graham, and others—acted in the face of equally challenging crises. To follow the examples set by these leaders:

✓ Acknowledge people's fears, then encourage them with resolve.

✓ Give people a role and a purpose.

✓ Encourage experimentation and learning.

✓ Manage your own and others' energy and emotions.

*Adapted from "Real Leaders Are Forged in Crisis" on hbr.org, April 3, 2020 (product #H05JEN).*

# Section 2

# MANAGING YOUR WORKFORCE

# FIFTEEN QUESTIONS ABOUT REMOTE WORK, ANSWERED

by Tsedal Neeley

T he coronavirus pandemic is expected to fundamentally change the way many organizations operate for the foreseeable future. As governments and businesses around the world tell those with symptoms to self-quarantine and everyone else to practice social distancing, remote work is our new reality. How do corporate leaders, managers, and individual workers make this sudden shift? Tsedal Neeley, a professor at Harvard

Business School, has spent two decades helping companies learn how to manage dispersed teams. In this edited Q&A, drawn from a recent *HBR* subscriber video call in which listeners were able to ask questions, she offers guidance on how to work productively at home, manage virtual meetings, and lead teams through this time of crisis.

**HBR:** *Are organizations prepared for this sudden transition?*

**NEELEY:** The scale and scope of what we're seeing, with organizations of 5,000 or 10,000 employees asking people to work from home very quickly, is unprecedented. So, no, organizations are not set up for this.

*What's the first thing that leaders and individual managers can do to help their employees get ready?*

Get the infrastructure right. Do people have the requisite technology or access to it? Who has a laptop? Will those who do [have laptops] be able to dial in to their organizations easily? Will they have the software they need to be able to do work, have conference calls, etc.? What about the employees who don't have laptops or mobile devices? How do you make sure that they have access to the resources they need to do work? Direct managers have to very quickly ensure that every employee has full access, so no one feels left behind.

### What should people who aren't accustomed to remote work do to get psychologically ready for it?

Develop rituals, and have a disciplined way of managing the day. Schedule a start time and an end time. Have a rhythm. Take a shower, get dressed, even if it's not what you'd usually wear to work, then get started on the day's activities. If you're used to moving physically, make sure you build that into your day. If you're an extrovert and accustomed to a lot of contact and collaboration with others, make sure that still happens. Ask yourself: How will I protect myself from feeling lonely or isolated and stay healthy, productive, and vibrant? Create that for yourself.

Remember that you might actually enjoy working from home. You can play the music you like. You can think flexibly about your time. It can be fun. As for managers, they need to check in on people. Make sure not only that they're set up but also that they have a rhythm to their day and contact with others. Ask: "What can I do to make sure that this sudden and quick transition is working for you?"

*How should those check-ins happen? As a group? In one-on-ones? Via phone calls? Or video chats?*

First, you should have a group conversation about the new state of affairs. Say, "Hey, folks, it's a different world. We don't know how long this is going to last. But I want to make sure you all feel that you have what you need." This should be followed by a team launch to jump-start this new way of working. Figure out: How often should we communicate? Should it be video, phone, or Slack/ Jive/Yammer? If you're not using one of those social media systems, should you? What's the best way for us to work together? You've got to help people understand how to do remote work and give them confidence that it will work.

Once those things are sorted out, meet with your group at least once a week. In a remote environment, frequency of contact cannot go down. If you're used to having meetings, continue to do so. In fact, contact should probably go up for the whole team and its members. Newer employees, those working on critical projects, and people who need more contact will require extra one-on-ones. Remember, too, that you can do fun things virtually: happy hour, coffee breaks, lunch together. All these things can help maintain the connections you had at the office. There's ample research showing that virtual teams can be completely equal to colocated ones in terms of trust and collaboration. It just requires discipline.

*How does working from home affect psychological health? What can employers do to make sure that people are staying focused, committed, and happy?*

People lose the unplanned watercooler or cappuccino conversations with colleagues in remote work. These are actually big and important parts of the workday that have a direct impact on performance. How do we create those virtually? For some groups and individuals, it will be constant instant messaging. For others, it will be live phone conversations or video conferences. Some people might want to use WhatsApp, WeChat, or Viber. A manager can encourage those types of contact points for psychological health. People are not going to be able to figure these things out organically. You've got to coach them. One more piece of advice: Exercise. It's critical for mental well-being.

*What are the top three things that leaders can do to create a good remote culture?*

There are more than 10,000 books in the English language on Amazon on virtuality and how to lead remotely or at a distance. Why is that? Because this is very difficult to do, and managers have to actively work on it. Number one, make sure that team members constantly feel like they know what's going on. You need to communicate what's happening at the organizational level because, when they're at home, they feel like they've been extracted from the mothership. They wonder what's happening at the company, with clients, and with common objectives. The communication around those is extremely important. So you're emailing more, sharing more.

During this period, people will also start to get nervous about revenue goals and other deliverables. You'll have to make sure they feel like they're going to be okay. Another thing is to ensure that no members feel like they have less access to you than others. When people are at home, their imaginations begin to go wild. So you have to be available to everyone equally. Finally, when you run your group meetings, aim for inclusion, and balance the airtime, so everyone feels seen and heard.

*How will these changes affect productivity?*

Productivity does not have to go down at all. It can be maintained, even enhanced, because commutes and office distractions are gone. Of course, you might be at home with your partner or kids, and those issues will need to be worked out. Another problem might be your ability to resolve problems quickly when you can't meet in person, in real time. That might create delays. But other than that, I don't see productivity going down. There's robust evidence showing that it shouldn't change.

*If the social-distancing policies go on for a while, how do you measure your employees' productivity and eventually review them on that work?*

I'll say this to every manager out there: You have to trust your employees. This is an era and a time in which we have to heed Ernest Hemingway's advice: "The best way to find out if you can trust somebody is to trust them." You can't see what people are doing. But equip them in the right ways, give them the tasks, check on them like you've always done, and hope they produce in the ways you want them to. You can't monitor the process, so your review will have to be outcome based. But there's no reason to believe that, in this new environment, people won't do the work that they've been assigned. Remote work has been around for a very long time. And today we have all the technologies we need to not only do work but also collaborate. We have enterprise-wide social media tools that allow us to store and capture data, to have one-to-many conversations, to share best practices, and to learn.

*Let's talk about virtual meetings. What are some best practices, beyond the general advice to clarify your purpose, circulate an agenda, prepare people to be called on, and so forth?*

First, you have to have some explicit ground rules. Say, "Folks, when we have these meetings, we do it in a nice way, we turn off our phones, we don't check emails or multitask." I highly recommend video conferencing if you have the ability to do that. When people are able to see one another, it really makes a difference. And then you trust people to follow the ground rules.

Number two, because you no longer have watercooler conversations, and people might be just learning how to work from home, spend the first six to seven minutes of a meeting checking in. Don't go straight to your agenda items. Instead, go around and ask everyone, "How are you guys doing?" Start with whoever is the newest or lowest-status person or the one who usually speaks the least. You should share as well, so that you're modeling the behavior. After that, introduce the key things you want to talk about and again model what you want to see, whether it's

connecting, asking questions, or even just using your pre-
ferred technology, like Zoom or Skype for Business.

The last thing is you have to follow up these virtual
meetings with redundant communication to ensure that
people have heard you and that they're okay with the outcome. Say you have a video conference about a topic. You
follow it up with an email or a Slack message. You should
have multiple touchpoints through various media to continue the trail of conversation.

*And how do you facilitate highly complex or
emotionally charged conversations when people
aren't face to face?*

You can only raise one or two of these topics because
you don't have the time or opportunity to work things
through after the meeting. You can't just walk to people's
offices to follow up. So be very thoughtful about what
you bring up and when and how you do it. But you can
still have these conversations. Allowing people to dis-
agree in order to sharpen the team's thinking is a very
positive thing. Sometimes, in virtual environments,
people don't feel psychologically safe, so they might
not speak up when they should. And so you might even
want to generate or model a little disagreement—always

over work, tasks or processes, of course, never anything personal.

*In light of various day-care and school closings, how do you discuss children and child care?*

Leaders should be prepared for that conversation and to help people think those issues through. The blurring of boundaries between work and home has suddenly come upon us, so managers have got to develop the skills and policies to support their teams. This might involve being more flexible about the hours in which employees work. You don't have to eat lunch at twelve p.m. You might walk your dog at two p.m. Things are much more fluid, and managers just have to trust that employees will do their best to get their work done.

*We've talked about internal communication, but what advice do you have for people in client-facing functions?*

We've been seeing virtual sales calls and client engagements. You do the exact same things. Here, it's even more important to use visual media. Take whatever you would be doing face to face and keep doing it. Maybe you can't wine and dine. But you can do a lot. Be creative.

*What do you do in an organization where you have a mix of both blue- and white-collar workers? Or for those colleagues who aren't properly equipped?*

The organizations have to figure out a way to support those workers—some kind of collective action to help them because otherwise you're completely isolating people who are critically important to your operation. I would put together a task force, and I would find solutions to keep them connected and ensure that they still feel valued. And include them in the planning.

*If you sense that, despite your best efforts, an employee is struggling—not focused, lonely—what can you do?*

When you see the signs—like fewer emails or more inhibition in group conversations—talk to them. Increase contact and encourage others to as well. Understand where they are. And get them what they need. Organizations should also make sure to have employee assistance services at this time. When you're suddenly taking away people's regular routines and connection with others, and it's open ended, some will struggle and need extra help. I would add that every CEO of every organization needs to be much more visible right now—through video conferencing or taped record-ings—to give people confidence, calm them down, and be healers- or hope-givers-in-chief.

*Do you see this crisis changing the way all teams and organizations operate going forward?*

I think it's going to broaden their repertoires. Organ-izations, teams, and people will experiment more with virtual work. Many of them have always wanted to test it as a way of expanding their reach or labor force. It's not that people are going to permanently adopt this new for-mat of work, but this experience will expand everyone's capacity. If there's a tiny positive aspect to this mess we're finding ourselves in, it's that we're developing certain skills that could be helpful in the future. That's my deep-est hope.

**TAKEAWAYS**

Remote work is now our reality. We can all make the best of this sudden shift by improving the ways we work productively at home, manage virtual meetings, and lead teams through this time of crisis.

✓ To create a positive remote work culture, ensure that your team members always feel as though they know what's going on and they have access to you. Aim for inclusion, and balance airtime in meetings so everyone feels seen and heard.

✓ To gauge your employees' productivity, you'll have to trust them. Give them tasks, and believe that they'll produce the way they always do. Your review of their work will have to be based on outcomes.

✓ Raise only one or two highly emotional or complex topics in any meeting or conversation; it's harder to follow up and find a way to diffuse tension remotely than in person. But recognize that difficult conversations are still essential, and allow people to feel the psychological safety needed to express disagreement.

*Adapted from "15 Questions About Remote Work, Answered" on hbr.org, March 16, 2020 (product #H05HK4).*

# 5

# HOW TO MANAGE CORONAVIRUS LAYOFFS WITH COMPASSION

by Rebecca Knight

A s the coronavirus pandemic continues to evolve, the damage to the job market looks likely to be deep and long-lasting. Managers are not only dealing with the stress and sadness of having to let go of a large number of their workers; many of them also feel underlying anxiety about their own positions. Even if laying off employees is the only way to keep the organization running, how do you handle your feelings of guilt and sadness? How should you deliver the news when you can't meet face to face? What should you say to your employees who remain? And what can you do to manage fear about your own future?

## What the Experts Say

Laying off employees is difficult in normal times, but amidst the Covid-19 global health crisis, the task is "emotionally and cognitively overwhelming," according to Joshua Margolis, a professor at Harvard Business School. "This experience for most of us is unfathomable," he says. "There's a great deal of uncertainty, and people's minds are whirring." As a manager charged with dismissing a wide swath of employees, "you're pulled in different directions. Your heart goes out to people, but you have a responsibility to the organization." That tension is magnified when you're also worried about your own fate, says Kenneth Freeman, Dean Emeritus at Boston University's Questrom School of Business. "You're human and you're going to have a lot of those two a.m. moments," he says. But the key is to try as best you can to separate your personal worries from the task at hand. "In your role as a manager, you need to be there for your people." Here are some recommendations.

## Leaders: Reflect on Whether Layoffs Are Needed

If you're the one making the decisions about layoffs, Margolis recommends asking yourself one question: Is downsizing your workforce truly necessary? The impulse to cut costs is understandable, but "this is not a periodic recession." Rather, the pandemic represents "an exceptional historic moment that will end up being pivotal for the economy and for people's communities, careers, and lives," and it might "warrant a different response." As a leader, you need to spark "resourceful, creative thinking about how your organization can save as many jobs as possible." Freeman suggests gathering your management team and asking, "Can we make sacrifices elsewhere? What are our other options to reduce costs?" Your goal is to think broadly about how you distribute the widespread negative consequences of Covid-19. "Laying off people should be the last resort," he says. And if you must do layoffs, make every effort to "avoid multiple rounds" of cuts.

## Gather Information

If you decide layoffs are necessary, or others have made that decision for you, then make sure you're prepared before you reach out to the affected employees. Figure out "how and when you will deliver the news to your employees on an individual basis" and what the message will consist of, says Freeman. People are likely going to have a lot of questions about the timing, their benefits, and severance. These conversations may need to happen fast, but you'll have a better chance of easing your own and the employee's anxiety if you can provide them with answers about what happens next. Reach out to HR, your legal department, and any other senior leaders who might be able to help you prepare answers to questions such as "When will I get my last paycheck?" and "What happens to my 401(k)?"

## Understand Your Limitations

Even if you've presided over layoffs in the past, overseeing them during the coronavirus outbreak will be different for one key reason: They probably won't take place in person because of social-distancing measures. What's more, you need to have a highly private conversation at a time when privacy is difficult to achieve. "We all have families under foot and lots of things going on," says Margolis. He suggests asking your employee, "Is there a time when I can get 15 minutes of your full attention?" Be forewarned: You may get pushback. They may anticipate what's coming, and "some people aren't going to have the psychological wherewithal to deal with it," he says. In this case, he recommends saying something like, "Can you let me know when you're ready to have this conversation so I can tell you the next steps?"

## Set the Right Tone

If you have to deliver the message remotely, Freeman says that you must take extra care to break the news "with empathy and compassion." Your aim is to "treat people with dignity, fairness, and respect." Even though you may worry that you, too, might get laid off, this particular termination is not about you. "This is not a time for you to take up space," says Margolis. Don't succumb to your insecurities by saying something like, "This is really hard for me." At the same time, don't "totally detach from your humanity" so that you "become a mechanical robot." Instead, find a way "to engage your emotion" and cultivate a "calm and low-key" manner. Ideally, you will have the conversation via video link so that you can make eye contact with the other person. If the conversation takes place on the phone, free yourself of all distractions. As Margolis says, "Be fully present and listen."

## Be Direct and Human

Your message should be "clear, concise, and unequivocal," says Margolis—for instance, "I'm sorry, but at the end of next week we are terminating your job." Imparting an "expeditious, direct message can feel cold, but it allows the other person to process what you're saying," he says. Express gratitude for their hard work and dedication. Then offer a short and simple explanation about the economic conditions that led to the layoff. "Stress that this is not about a specific job performance," says Freeman. "This is not the employee's fault. This is about a global circumstance that none of us created." Acknowledge, too, that one of the difficult things about being laid off during this crisis is that coworkers won't get a chance to say good-bye in person. For a lot of people, "colleagues are part of their extended family." Try to convey the message that "we all care about you."

## Offer Assistance—but Don't Overpromise

Freeman recommends "being readily available" and willing to provide "support and counsel" to your employee, even after the initial conversation. Recognize that this person may need time to process the news and may have questions for you later. "They might come back to reconnect or seek your advice," Freeman says. Be helpful. Provide information regarding where your employee should go for government benefits. Offer ideas about job opportunities at other organizations. Offer to serve as a reference. But, cautions Margolis, "Don't overcommit to things you can't deliver." For instance, "You may feel tempted to say, 'As things get clearer, and the economy improves, you're on our list to come back,'" he says. But no one has that kind of foresight. "Don't sugarcoat, and don't give false hope."

## Be Transparent

In times like these, your remaining employees will look to you for comfort—and an explanation, says Freeman. "The survivors are going to be worried about their jobs," he says. The fact is, "No one knows where this is going to end," so the "onus is on you to be as transparent as possible." He recommends you hold an "Ask Me Anything" session—an open forum of sorts—so that "rumors don't take over." You will need "a succinct explanation for why the layoffs were necessary," says Margolis. He recommends saying something like, "The organization is facing a challenge unlike anything it has ever faced. Let me tell you what we did, why we did it, and how we can move on." Then it's up to you to "absorb their tension and agitation" and listen to their concerns. You need to "exude a commitment to continue to move forward," he says.

## Vent (Selectively)

This is an excruciatingly stressful time for everyone, and managers often bear an extra burden, says Freeman. "You feel responsible for the livelihoods of your team and for the health and well-being of their families," he says. One of the many ways that people "cope with turbulence" is by going to routines and rituals, says Margolis. But because of widespread lockdowns and shelter-in-place orders, our routines "have been disrupted." It's critical, therefore, that you have "a place where you can vent, release tension, and where you deal with your worries." Find someone else you can talk to—maybe a peer, a mentor, or a colleague at a different organization. "It's okay to articulate in certain circles that you don't know about your own future and that unleashes worry." But be selective and cautious about how much stress and emotion you show to your team. "All eyes are on you" to provide a path forward.

## Focus on Your Well-Being

Finally, take care of yourself, says Margolis. "Hopefully, this is the only time you face something of this magnitude. But it's unlikely to be the only time you face a challenge during a period of great uncertainty. The best coping mechanism for when you can't anticipate what's in store for you is self-care." Eat healthy, wholesome food; get regular exercise; try meditating; get plenty of sleep at night; read a good book. A little perspective helps too. After all, "You are not alone," says Freeman. Unfortunately, "there are a lot of supervisors going through this."

TAKEAWAYS

Laying off employees is difficult in normal times, but amidst the Covid-19 global health crisis, the task may be emotionally and cognitively overwhelming. Following a few important practices can help you minimize the emotional toll on your employees and yourself.

✓ Because you will deliver the message remotely, take extra care to break the news with empathy and compassion. Treat people with dignity, fairness, and respect.

✓ Offer a short explanation about the economic conditions that led to the layoff. Stress that the dismissal is not the employee's fault. Rather, it's the result of a global circumstance none of them created.

✓ Don't overcommit. Provide support and counsel to the people you've laid off, but don't promise things you can't deliver.

✓ Even if you're worried that you, too, might lose your job, don't make the situation about you. Find someone to vent to—a peer or mentor perhaps—and an outlet for your stress.

*Adapted from "How to Manage Coronavirus Layoffs with Compassion" on hbr.org, April 7, 2020 (product #H05JOY).*

# 6

# YOUR EMPLOYEE TESTED POSITIVE FOR COVID-19. WHAT DO YOU DO?

by Alisa Cohn

**A**ll leaders are trying to find their footing right now. You are probably shoring up your business plan, situating your team, and juggling your own constellation of remote working arrangements—possibly alongside your spouse and children. On top of that, you may face a test you probably couldn't have imagined a few weeks ago: when one of your employees tells you they have tested positive for Covid-19. If you haven't dealt with that already, you almost certainly will.

This is a particularly complex challenge. Not only does the moment call for sensitivity and humanity, but it also requires you to act quickly as a manager. As an executive coach, I have coached many senior leaders on high-stakes matters that, like this, require both decisive action and emotional intelligence. Here are my recommendations for how to approach this situation, whether your employees are currently working from home or continuing to go into a workplace.

First, when the employee brings you the news, *express sympathy.* Even if the person's symptoms are mild, they are likely to be anxious about what might happen or whether they might have spread the virus to their family or coworkers. Let the employee share their feelings. As you talk with them, clearly communicate that they can count on you and the team to be supportive. You could say, for example, "I know that this is a scary thing to deal with. I am here for you if you need to talk, and certainly I understand that you may not be able to work for a little while or that your productivity may go down. Don't worry about that; I understand what you're dealing with."

Next, connect with your HR partner. *You need to act quickly to minimize the risk of the disease spreading.* At this point, most HR departments should have some protocols in place, and you will want to utilize their support and guidance.

Minimally, you will need to *ask the employee which coworkers they have been in "close contact" with* in the prior two weeks. (The U.S. Centers for Disease Control and Prevention [CDC] defines "close contact" as "a person that has been within six feet of the infected employee for a prolonged period of time.") If everyone in your company has been working from home during the last two weeks, it may be unlikely that the infected person has had contact with a coworker, but you should still ask. You should alert those who have been in close contact with the employee as soon as possible, repeat the advice given on the CDC website for their situation, and, of course, direct them to their own doctors. The law is clear about confidentiality here: You should tell everyone who was possibly exposed to the positive employee at work without revealing that employee's identity.

You will need to decide whether it should be you or the HR partner who connects with any close contacts the employee has had. Since this is a sensitive topic, *it's ideal to alert the coworkers by video or phone.* But time matters here—if you can't reach them personally, email them with "important action required" in the subject heading.

Either way, *your message is the same*: "Someone in our workplace has tested positive for Covid-19, and they have identified you as a close contact according to the CDC definition. We are here to support you. If you are at work, please prepare to leave as quickly as you can. Once you get home—or if you are already working from home—find a place to self-isolate, monitor yourself for any symptoms, and talk to your doctors. How can I support you in doing all of this?"

*You can expect people in the close-contact group to be nervous* and ask a lot of questions, especially if it's the first time they are receiving such news. Since several days have passed between their exposure to the Covid-positive colleague, they may ask you if their family is at risk. Don't speculate. You are not a doctor. Instead, refer them to their own physician and to the CDC website. What you *can* do is reassure them that the company, and you, will be supportive.

*Follow up this conversation by email.* It's likely that the person you were talking to was feeling overwhelmed and did not catch everything you said. A written follow-up is always good practice, if only to help keep track of the process inside your company.

Once you have spoken with both the employee who tested positive and their close contacts, consider alerting others in the workplace. The message you send here will showcase how your company treats people, so it's important to be transparent and calming.

The ways you communicate this can vary. If the company is a startup with under a few hundred employees, it may be appropriate to communicate the news to everyone in an all-hands meeting. If your company is much larger, it's most important to communicate to the affected department or division. *Respect the confidentiality of both the positive-tested employee and anyone in the close-contact group.* Then simply give them the facts: "The person tested positive on a certain date and is now self-isolating. The close contacts have been told and were asked to leave the workplace and self-isolate. If you were not already told that you were a close contact, then you are not one. If you have questions about Covid-19 or your situation, please call your doctor and look at the CDC website. The company is here to support everyone during this difficult time, and we all send our best wishes to the people affected."

Finally, *it is helpful for a senior leader, perhaps even the CEO, to check in on any employee affected by the coronavirus.* A CEO whom I coach called every one of their employees who tested positive as well as their close contacts—even if they showed no symptoms—just to check in, a gesture they universally appreciated. If the cases at your company start to increase dramatically, it will not be realistic for the CEO to call all these people. However, senior leaders can and should step in to make as many calls as possible so employees who are affected feel cared for during a difficult time.

These are not easy times for anyone, and it is a crucial job of leaders to reassure their employees and keep up their spirits. An employee who reports a positive Covid-19 test requires a sensitive and rapid response. That will help everyone who works for you feel more secure and be more able to focus on the important work at your company right now.

## TAKEAWAYS

When an employee informs you that they have tested positive for Covid-19, the moment calls for sensitivity and humanity, but it also requires you to act quickly as a manager.

✓ Express empathy to your employee and identify which other employees they have been in close contact with. Connect with your HR partner for guidance, and inform those at risk by phone or video if possible.

✓ While your employees will likely have questions, don't speculate. Encourage them to talk to their doctor.

✓ Respect the confidentiality of the employee who tested positive and of the close contacts.

✓ Encourage senior leaders to check in with any Covid-positive employees. It is a gesture that will be universally appreciated.

*Adapted from "Your Employee Tested Positive for Covid-19. What Do You Do?" on hbr.org, March 30, 2020 (product #H05IX6).*

# 7

# HOW CAN'T-CLOSE RETAILERS ARE KEEPING WORKERS SAFE

by Sarah Kalloch and Zeynep Ton

**W**orkers at grocery stores, pharmacies, convenience stores, and other "can't-close" retail businesses are working overtime and risking their own health to keep the rest of us in food, medicine, and toilet paper. The companies they work for need to take care of them in order to keep both them and us safe.

It isn't easy to balance well-stocked shelves with the safety of employees and customers, and there isn't much time to learn. So there will definitely be mistakes along the way. But based on our research and work, we think the operational practices and values of the retailers we call "good-jobs companies" can provide guidance to others. This is no coincidence. The various things that good-jobs companies do differently from other companies are all designed to make their frontline employees so valuable and productive that their contributions more than repay the greater wages, benefits, and training they receive. The resulting dedication and adaptiveness are exactly what companies need in order to cope with the Covid-19 pandemic.

Below are some of the practices of good-jobs companies—in particular, Costco, Mercadona, H-E-B, and Mud Bay—that can be adopted to keep customers and employees safe right now.

## Focus and Simplify to Reduce Workloads

Some retailers are experiencing peak demand around the clock, which makes it hard to maintain social distancing and to make time for safety procedures such as sanitizing shelves. Normally, cleaning a dusty shelf may not be as important as tending to the 100 people lined up at the checkout. Right now, however, it is. So now is the time to reduce workload by rationalizing the product line, limiting shopping hours, and clearly explaining why you're doing so to customers (so they don't bug the employees) and to employees (so they can explain to customers).

Mercadona, Spain's largest grocery chain, has instructed staff and has used social media to tell customers to shop quickly, to have only one person per family in the store, and not to hoard. Costco closed its food court, optical department, and hearing-aid department. It is not accepting returns on high-demand items like toilet paper, paper towels, Lysol, and rice—both to simplify work and to discourage hoarding.

## Adopt Clear Safety Standards

Given the virulence of Covid-19 and the difficulties of maintaining and enforcing safety precautions, especially in retail stores with hundreds of anxious shoppers, reducing the risk to zero is impossible. That said, retailers need to create and communicate clear standards for sanitizing stores, distribution centers, and trucks; for social distancing; for handwashing and personal protection; for surveillance to identify potential illness in employees; and for new ways of working (for instance, switching from huddles to different modes of communication, or creating smaller work groups in distribution centers).

Companies with high employee turnover and weak unit managers with short tenures—a description that fits most retail chains and online retailers—will have a hard time adhering to safety standards. Good-jobs companies, on the other hand, already excel at creating and conforming to strong standards by using input from the front lines and then providing those front lines with the necessary tools and enough time. Costco, for example, has strong, empowered middle managers and dedicated frontline staff who all take high standards seriously. That puts Costco in a strong position to enforce novel and strict standards related to closing every other register for social distancing and limiting the number of members who enter. At Mud Bay, a pet store chain in the Northwest, door greeters ask customers to wash their hands at an outdoor station before entering the store and to stay six feet apart once inside. Staff are empowered to ask a customer who refuses to practice social distancing to leave the store.

## Empower and Continuously Improve

Covid-19 will call for new everyday work processes and will not wait around for a cautious rollout. The

continuous-improvement culture at good-jobs companies enables them to innovate faster and better. Early in
the pandemic, Costco, Mercadona, and H-E-B, for example, placed plexiglass in checkouts to keep employees safe. Costco repurposed the plexiglass from seafood
displays. Mud Bay quickly rolled out curbside pickup,
which went from 0% of sales to more than 6% in five
days. CEO Lars Wulff said his stores could do this
quickly because of a stable workforce that was already
empowered to make decisions. This is crucial, because
many stores have different setups and local customer
needs.

## Operate with Slack

Good-jobs companies staff their stores with more hours
of labor than the expected workload, which enables
them to react to changes in demand or supply. Given the
increase in customer demand and additional callouts
due to illness, operating with slack is especially important now. It isn't just Amazon that's suddenly hiring in
a big way.

Companies may also need to repurpose roles to create more capacity. H-E-B, a Texas supermarket chain, is
adding an extra manager in charge of Covid-19 response

who ensures that the stores are sanitized twice a day, maintains regular food sanitation, and monitors lines at food counters and checkouts to ensure social distancing.

Good-jobs companies also operate with financial slack. This means making sure they have the money on hand to deal with unforeseen events. In 2008, when the world economy was collapsing, Mercadona had enough cash on hand to pay bonuses to its workers. Its leaders knew they were going to need to ask more of those workers as the company innovated to cut prices for struggling customers. Retailers are asking even more of their employees now.

## Show Respect

Respect is not a luxury when you're asking people to risk themselves. It is time for all retailers to show respect by prioritizing workers' safety, offering decent pay and benefits, giving them the tools and resources they need to do a good job, and recognizing them when they do. Good-jobs companies already do that, but Mercadona is now boosting pay by 20%, and Mud Bay, H-E-B, and Costco (which already pays among the highest wages in retail) are paying workers two dollars more per hour during the crisis. An empowered Costco warehouse manager in Massachusetts is providing meals for his team. QuikTrip's CEO is visiting stores to show solidarity, recognize good work, and communicate that their jobs are safe (but adheres to recommended social-distancing and sanitizing practices while doing so). Home office leaders at Sam's Club are taking shifts in the stores to support their colleagues, which may also help them better understand the pressures of operating in this kind of environment so they can craft stronger policies moving forward.

## Prioritize Customers and Employees over Shareholders

All these interventions to keep customers and employees safe cost extra money in the short term. Mercadona is giving out gloves to customers and hiring private security guards to help with crowd control and take some of the load off store managers. Good-jobs companies are able to implement these changes more quickly because they already have a culture of doing the right thing and prioritizing people over shareholders.

A Costco employee told us, "The dedication and drive that Costco employees have sets us apart from everybody else. During these times, our true colors have really shone." That dedication and drive didn't just spring up under pressure. They are the carefully cultivated results of a specific set of practices. If Covid-19 draws attention to the long-term value of good-jobs practices, it will have had at least one positive impact.

TAKEAWAYS

One of the biggest challenges that essential retailers face is keeping their workers and customers safe from Covid-19. Learning along the way, adhering to strong standards, and dedication to maintaining safety are essential. Studying the longtime practices and values of a group of model retailers, including Costco, Mercadona, H-E-B, and Mud Bay, can help companies ride out the storm:

✓ Focus and simplify to reduce workloads.

✓ Adopt clear safety standards.

✓ Empower employees to continuously improve.

✓ Operate with slack.

✓ Show respect.

✓ Prioritize customers and employees over shareholders.

*Adapted from "How Can't-Close Retailers Are Keeping Workers Safe" on hbr.org, March 30, 2020 (product #H05IKO).*

# Section 3

# MANAGING YOURSELF

8

# HOW TO MANAGE YOUR STRESS WHEN THE SKY IS FALLING

by Michael Gervais

It's natural to feel stressed right now. As we try to navigate our new normal, we're worried about getting sick or losing our jobs, we're inundated with news about death tolls and an economic recession, and we're isolated from coworkers, friends, and family.

Stress helps prepare us to meet the demands and challenges of our environment—up to a point. The chain of rapidly occurring neurochemical and neuroelectrical reactions can sharpen attention and our ability to assess our surroundings, motivate us, and even briefly boost our immune system. But it's designed to be a short-term response—to last for minutes or hours, not days or weeks.

When our stress system stays activated for a prolonged period, it can suppress our adaptive immune systems and make us more vulnerable to viral infections. That's why we need to manage our stress now more than ever. Like the elite athletes I work with, who can control their physiological and mental arousal, we need to employ psychological skills to move ourselves into our activation sweet spot to perform well and live well. Those who understand how to use their mind to manage stress look for the optimal state, where they are "switched on" but not wound too tight.

We may not have control over our circumstances, but we do have control over our minds. Even if you think you're relatively calm, know that stress is a stealthy and powerful adversary. It can hit you out of nowhere. So we should all be employing mental skills and practices to get us through this trying time.

## Breathe

A mindfulness practice allows us to have space from our cognition and emotion so we can see things as they really are. Rather than being anxious, we can see that we're experiencing anxiousness. There's a big difference.

Start from the moment you wake up. In a recent video, my colleague the former Olympian Courtney Thompson offered advice on how to set our minds right each morning. Instead of reaching for your phone, checking the news, or scrolling through social media, try this:

1. Take one really long, deep breath—more than 10 seconds—and try to exhale longer than you inhale. Express one thought of gratitude. Don't just check a box. Are there people in your life that are stepping up? Is your family healthy? Try to really feel it. It's not an exercise in thinking; it's an integration between thinking and feeling.

2. Set your intention for the day. I don't mean your goals or to-dos. I mean, what type of person are you going to be today? An intention represents a commitment to carrying out an action in the future. Are you going to show up for others? Be calm and controlled for family, friends, strangers, and colleagues? This is an exercise in imagery, seeing yourself at your best.

3. Pull off the sheets and put your feet on the ground. Take a moment to feel your feet on the floor. Be

where your feet are. This is a primer to mentally and physically start your day in the present moment.

No matter what's happening, remember that you're in control of your thoughts (well, at least the ones you're aware of). You can decide what you'd like your first thoughts each day to be. Choose well.

If you're feeling unfocused or anxious during the day, take eight minutes and just breathe, observing your passing thoughts without judgment and bringing your attention back to your breath when those thoughts grab your attention. If you become distracted, refocus on your next breath. Try it. There's no right or wrong way to practice.

## Eat and Sleep Well

Self-care during times of high stress is essential. It sounds simple and obvious, but when we're in survival mode, many of us don't take good enough care of ourselves.

Great sleep is crucial. Recently, on my podcast *Finding Mastery*, I spoke with Matthew Walker, a sleep expert and Professor of Neuroscience and Psychology at the University of California, Berkeley. For optimal sleep, he suggests going to bed at the same time each night. Your brain thrives on regularity—not Netflix.

But if you're stressed out, you may have trouble falling or staying asleep. If you run into trouble, Walker suggests "walking it off." I suggest one of the following three tactics: Brush your teeth (to reignite a Pavlovian, it's-time-to-go-to-sleep response), read a book (the more boring the better), or jot down your thoughts on a pad of paper (not your phone!) until you feel sleepy.

Try to wake up at the same time each morning, too—even if you had a bad night's sleep. Regularity will keep your circadian rhythms in check.

Eat and hydrate well. In times of high stress, our bodies crave sugar, starches, and salt. But research has found that people who have a healthy diet are less prone to infections. Eat colorfully. Dark and leafy vegetables (sorry, candies and chocolate don't count) are an efficient way to feed the energy needs of your immune system. And drink plenty of water. It flushes toxins from your body.

## Create Connection

During uncertainty, we typically gravitate toward our tribe for comfort and support. In this instance, we are being asked to separate from the community, to shelter in place, to keep our social distance. If left unchecked, social isolation can lead to loneliness, which can have drastic effects on our mental and physical health.

Separation doesn't have to mean isolation. Take this time to really connect with others. Tell them how valuable they are to you. Send messages of praise to your coworkers. Tell your family how much you love them. Make a list of people you want to call, to thank them for making a difference in your life. And don't only broadcast your own concerns. Be curious about how others are doing—and truly listen. Do it today.

This is a time to practice compassion. Almost everyone will be affected by the social, physical, and economic dislocation of the pandemic. Recognize that we are all in this together. There is no "other."

Shake things up. Partake in Instagram dance parties. Sing. Or make music together. Italy offers a beautiful example of creating joy and connection while in lockdown. People have started singing from their balconies, out their windows, and across rooftops at appointed times, coordinating their efforts via social media. *Viva l'Italia!*

This isn't the time to be overly worried about what others think of you. We're all in this—together—and if there were ever a time to let loose, this is it. Connecting with others, and being open and vulnerable, is what's going to get us through.

# Find Purpose

As the news gets worse, and we go about our everyday routines, you may find yourself thinking that your life and work lack fire. So try anchoring this remarkable period in a purpose larger than yourself. You get to decide the story you tell yourself. When we have an orientation beyond ourselves, it makes us more resilient in the face of challenges.

Victor Frankl, the Austrian neurologist and psychiatrist, survived four concentration camps, an experience that profoundly deepened his understanding of man. Frankl learned that our main drive or motivation in life is neither pleasure nor power but meaning. Frankl wrote, "Life is never made unbearable by circumstances, only by lack of meaning and purpose." Of his experience at the camps, he wrote, "Those who [were] oriented toward a meaning to be fulfilled by them in the future were most likely to survive."

For inspiration, take note of the people who are serving the greater good in response to the crisis. Some are helping the less fortunate in their communities. Others are using this as a teaching moment for their children. That's living—and leading—from a place of purpose. You can do the same.

As you forge ahead, and things get tough, remember that your most significant ally lies inside you: your mind. So take care if it—for your own health and the health of others.

While you may not have control over your circumstances, you do have control over your mind. There are a number of mental skills and practices you can use to manage stress in a crisis:

- ✓ **Breathe.** It begins when you wake up. Start with one long deep breath, set your intention for the day, and take a moment to really feel your feet on the floor.

- ✓ **Eat and sleep well.** Establish a regular circadian rhythm. Eat colorfully, and hydrate. The healthier we eat, the less prone we are to infections.

- ✓ **Create connection.** Separation doesn't mean you have to be isolated from others. Tell people how valuable they are to you. Send messages of praise to your coworkers. Let your family know how much you love them.

✓ **Find purpose.** You get to decide the story you tell yourself. When you have an orientation toward some purpose beyond yourself, it will make you more resilient in the face of challenges.

*Adapted from "How to Manage Your Stress When the Sky Is Falling" on hbr.org, April 10, 2020 (product #H05J63).*

# 9

# THREE TIPS TO AVOID WORKING-FROM-HOME BURNOUT

by Laura M. Giurge and Vanessa K. Bohns

**M**illions around the globe have made a sudden transition to remote work amid the Covid-19 pandemic. Not surprisingly, this has some employers concerned about maintaining employee productivity. But what they really should be concerned about in this unprecedented situation is a longer-term risk: employee burnout.

The risk is substantial. The lines between work and nonwork are blurring in new and unusual ways, and many employees who are working remotely for the first time are likely to struggle to preserve healthy boundaries between their professional and personal lives. To signal their loyalty, devotion, and productivity, they may feel they have to work all the time. Afternoons will blend with evenings, weekdays will blend with weekends, and little sense of time off will remain. It's possible that some employees may be asked to continue working remotely for several months.

Lots of research suggests that drawing lines between our professional and personal lives is crucial, especially for our mental health. But it's difficult, even in the best of circumstances. In no small measure, that's because the knowledge economy has radically transformed what it means to be an "ideal worker."

Our research has shown that workers often unintentionally make it hard for their supervisors, colleagues, and employees to maintain boundaries. One way they do so is by sending work emails outside office hours. In five studies involving more than 2,000 working adults, we found that senders of after-hours work emails underestimate how compelled receivers feel to respond right away, even when such emails are not urgent.

Covid-19 might amplify these pressures. Even for employees who have a natural preference to separate their work and personal lives, the current circumstances may not allow them to do so. Many schools are closed, and day care may no longer be an option, placing additional burdens on working parents or low-income workers. Even companies that already encourage employees to work from home are likely to have some trouble supporting employees who face the many challenges of working at home in the presence of their families.

So how can employees continue to compartmentalize their work and nonwork lives, given the extraordinary situation that so many of us are in today? How can we "leave our work at the door" if we are no longer going out the door? What can employers, managers, and coworkers do to help one another cope?

Based on our research and the wider academic literature, here are some recommendations.

## Maintain Physical and Social Boundaries

In a classic paper, Blake Ashforth, of Arizona State University, described the ways in which people demarcate the transition from work to nonwork roles via "boundary-crossing activities."[1] Putting on your work clothes, commuting from home to work—these are physical and social indicators that something has changed. You've transitioned from "home you" to "work you."

Try to maintain these boundaries when working remotely. In the short term, it may be a welcome change not to have to catch an early train to work, or not to have to dress up for work—but both those things are boundary-crossing activities that can do you good, so don't abandon them altogether. Put on your work clothes every morning; casual Friday is fine, of course, but get yourself ready nonetheless. And consider replacing your morning commute with a walk to a nearby park, or even just around your apartment, before sitting down to work. Some workers have already come up with creative and lighthearted ways to maintain their usual work routines.

## Maintain Temporal Boundaries as Much as Possible

Maintaining temporal boundaries is critical for well-being and work engagement. This is particularly true when so many employees—and/or their colleagues—now face the challenge of integrating child-care or elder-care responsibilities into regular work hours. It's challenging even for employees without children or other family responsibilities, thanks to the mobile devices that keep our work with us at all times.

Sticking to a nine-to-five schedule may prove unrealistic. Employees need to find work-time budgets that function best for them. They also need be conscious and respectful that others might work at different times than they do. For some it might be during a child's nap; for others it might be when their partner is cooking dinner. Employees with or without children can create intentional work-time budgets by adding an "out of office" reply to their emails during certain hours of the day to focus on work. A less extreme response might be to just let others know that you may be slower than usual in replying, decreasing response expectations for others and yourself.

Creating clear temporal boundaries often depends on the ability to coordinate one's time with others. This calls for leaders to aid employees in structuring, coordinating, and managing the pace of work—perhaps by regularly holding virtual check-in meetings, or providing employees with tools to create virtual break rooms or work spaces. Throughout this period of disruption, keeping a sense of normality is key.

## Focus on Your Most Important Work

This is not the time for busy work. Workers should be devoting their energy to top-priority issues.

While working from home, employees often feel compelled to project the appearance of productivity, but this can lead them to work on tasks that are more immediate instead of more important—a tendency that research suggests is counterproductive in the long run, even if it benefits productivity in the short run. Employees, particularly those facing increased workloads as they juggle family and work tasks, should pay attention to prioritizing important work.

Working all the time, even on your most important tasks, isn't the answer. According to some estimates, the average knowledge worker is only productive on average three hours every day, and those hours should be free of interruptions or multitasking. Even before Covid-19, employees found it difficult to carve out three continuous hours to focus on their core work tasks. With work and family boundaries being removed, employees' time has never been more fragmented.

Employees who feel "on" all the time are at a higher risk of burnout when working from home than if they were going to the office as usual. In the long term, trying to squeeze in work and email responses whenever we have a few minutes to do so—during the kids' nap time, on the weekend, or by pausing a movie in the evening—is not only counterproductive but also detrimental to our well-being. We all need to find new ways to carve out nonwork time and mental space—and help others do the same.

These are just a few recommendations that can help workers maintain boundaries between their work and their personal life and thereby avoid burnout in the long run. Employees will need the flexibility to experiment with how to make their circumstances work for them in these unpredictable times.

TAKEAWAYS

The blurring of the boundaries between work time and personal time that comes with remote work can lead to burnout. Those who are new to remote work are at an even higher risk. How can we "leave our work at the door" if we are no longer going out the door? Research shows it is important to:

✓ Maintain physical and social boundaries. Putting on your work clothes and commuting are physical and social indicators to your mind that something has changed. Dress for the workday, and consider replacing your commute with a walk.

✓ Maintain boundaries on how you use your time. Use an "out of office" reply to messages during certain hours of the day to allow you periods of uninterrupted work.

✓ Focus on your most important work. While working from home, people often feel compelled to project the appearance of productivity, which may lead them to work on tasks that are more immediate instead of more important. Devote your energy to top-priority issues.

## NOTE

1. Blake E. Ashforth, Glen E. Kreiner, and Mel Fugate, "All in a Day's Work: Boundaries and Micro Role Transitions," *Academy of Management Review* 25, no. 3 (July 2000): 472–491.

*Adapted from "3 Tips to Avoid WFH Burnout" on hbr.org, April 3, 2020 (product #H05IX0).*

# 10

# THAT DISCOMFORT YOU'RE FEELING IS GRIEF

by Scott Berinato

S
ome of the *HBR* editorial staff met virtually not long ago—a screenful of faces in a scene becoming more common everywhere. We talked about the content we're commissioning in this harrowing time of a pandemic and how we can help people. But we also talked about how we were feeling. One colleague mentioned that what she felt was grief. Heads nodded in all the panes.

If we can name it, perhaps we can manage it. We turned to David Kessler for ideas on how to do that.

Kessler is the world's foremost expert on grief. He co-wrote with Elisabeth Kübler-Ross *On Grief and Grieving: Finding the Meaning of Grief Through the Five Stages of Loss*. His new book, *Finding Meaning: The Sixth Stage of Grief*, adds another stage to the process. Kessler also has worked for a decade in a three-hospital system in Los Angeles. He served on their biohazards team. His volunteer work includes being a Los Angeles Police Department Specialist Reserve for traumatic events as well as having served on the Red Cross's disaster services team. He is the founder of grief.com, which has over five million visits yearly from 167 countries.

Kessler shared his thoughts on why it's important to acknowledge the grief you may be feeling, how to manage it, and how he believes we will find meaning in it. The conversation is lightly edited for clarity.

**HBR:** *People are feeling any number of things right now. Is it right to call some of what they're feeling grief?*

**KESSLER:** Yes, and we're feeling a number of different griefs. We feel the world has changed, and it has. We know this is temporary, but it doesn't feel that way, and we realize things will be different. Just as going to the airport is forever different from how it was before 9/11, things will change, and this is the point at which they changed. The loss of normalcy, the fear of economic toll, the loss of connection. This is hitting us and we're grieving. Collectively. We are not used to this kind of collective grief in the air.

*You said we're feeling more than one kind of grief?*

Yes, we're also feeling anticipatory grief. Anticipatory grief is that feeling we get about what the future holds when we're uncertain. Usually it centers on death. We feel it when someone gets a dire diagnosis or when we have the normal thought that we'll lose a parent someday. Anticipatory grief is also more broadly imagined futures. There is a storm coming. There's something bad out there. With a virus, this kind of grief is so confusing for people. Our primitive mind knows something bad is happening, but you can't see it. This breaks our sense of safety. We're feeling that loss of safety. I don't think we've collectively lost our sense of general safety like this. Individually or as smaller groups, people have felt this. But all together, this is new. We are grieving on a micro and a macro level.

*What can individuals do to manage all this grief?*

Understanding the stages of grief is a start. But whenever I talk about the stages of grief, I have to remind people that the stages aren't linear and may not happen in this order. It's not a map, but it provides some scaffolding for this unknown world. There's denial, which we say a lot of early on: This virus won't affect us. There's anger: You're making me stay home and taking away my activities. There's bargaining: Okay, if I social distance for two weeks everything will be better, right? There's sadness: I don't know when this will end. And finally there's acceptance: This is happening; I have to figure out how to proceed.

Acceptance, as you might imagine, is where the power lies. We find control in acceptance. I can wash my hands. I can keep a safe distance. I can learn how to work virtually.

*When we're feeling grief there's that physical pain. And the racing mind. Are there techniques to deal with that to make it less intense?*

Let's go back to anticipatory grief. Unhealthy anticipatory grief is really anxiety, and that's the feeling you're talking about. Our mind begins to show us images. My parents getting sick. We see the worst scenarios. That's our minds being protective. Our goal is not to ignore those images or to try to make them go away—your mind won't let you do that, and it can be painful to try and force it. The goal is to find balance in the things you're thinking. If you feel the worst image taking shape, make yourself think of the best image. We all get a little sick, and the world continues. Not everyone I love dies. Maybe no one does, because we're all taking the right steps. Neither scenario should be ignored, but neither should dominate, either.

Anticipatory grief is the mind going to the future and imagining the worst. To calm yourself, you want to come into the present. This will be familiar advice to anyone who has meditated or practiced mindfulness, but people are always surprised at how prosaic this can be. You can name five things in the room. There's a computer, a chair, a picture of the dog, an old rug, and a coffee mug. It's that simple. Breathe. Realize that in the present moment, nothing you've anticipated has happened. In this moment, you're okay. You have food. You are not sick. Use your senses, and think about what they feel. The desk is hard. The blanket is soft. I can feel the breath coming into my nose. This really will work to dampen some of that pain.

You can also think about how to let go of what you can't control. What your neighbor is doing is out of your control. What is in your control is staying six feet away from them and washing your hands. Focus on that.

Finally, it's a good time to stock up on compassion. Everyone will have different levels of fear and grief, and it manifests in different ways. A coworker got very snippy with me the other day, and I thought, That's not like this person; that's how they're dealing with this. I'm seeing their fear and anxiety. So be patient. Think about who someone usually is and not who they seem to be in this moment.

One particularly troubling aspect of this pandemic is the open-endedness of it.

This is a temporary state. It helps to say it. I worked for 10 years in the hospital system. I've been trained for situations like this. I've also studied the 1918 flu pandemic. The precautions we're taking are the right ones. History tells us that. This is survivable. We will survive. This is a time to overprotect but not overreact.

And I believe we will find meaning in it. I've been honored that Elisabeth Kübler-Ross's family has given me permission to add a sixth stage to grief: meaning. I had talked to Elisabeth quite a bit about what came after acceptance. I did not want to stop at acceptance when I experienced some personal grief. I wanted meaning in those darkest hours. And I do believe we find light in those times. Even now people are realizing they can connect through technology. They are not as remote as they thought. They are realizing they can use their phones for long conversations. They're appreciating walks. I believe we will continue to find meaning now and when this is over.

*What do you say to someone who's read all this and
is still feeling overwhelmed with grief?*

Keep trying. There is something powerful about naming
this as grief. It helps us feel what's inside of us. So many
have told me in the past week, "I'm telling my coworkers
I'm having a hard time," or "I cried last night." When you
name it, you feel it, and it moves through you. Emotions
need motion. It's important we acknowledge what we go
through. One unfortunate by-product of the self-help
movement is we're the first generation to have feelings
about our feelings. We tell ourselves things like, I feel
sad, but I shouldn't feel that; other people have it worse.
We can—we should—stop at the first feeling. I feel sad.
Let me go for five minutes to feel sad. Your work is to feel
your sadness and fear and anger whether or not someone
else is feeling something. Fighting it doesn't help, because
your body is producing the feeling. If we allow the feelings to happen, they'll happen in an orderly way, and it
empowers us. Then we're not victims.

*In an orderly way?*

Yes. Sometimes we try not to feel what we're feeling
because we have this image of a "gang of feelings." If I
feel sad and let that in, it'll never go away. The gang of

bad feelings will overrun me. The truth is a feeling that moves through us. We feel it and it goes, and then we go to the next feeling. There's no gang out to get us. It's absurd to think we shouldn't feel grief right now. Let yourself feel the grief and keep going.

TAKEAWAYS

During this pandemic, we're feeling grief in a number of ways. Beyond fear of illness and loss of life, there is the loss of normalcy, the fear of economic toll, the loss of connection. Here are some things to remember about grief:

- ✓ Understanding grief is the first step in managing it. The classic stages of grief may not happen in order, but they are a scaffolding for helping you navigate your emotions.

- ✓ Allow yourself to feel your feelings—emotions need motion, and fighting them off doesn't help. If we allow the feelings to happen, they'll occur in an orderly way, which empowers us.

✓ Anticipatory grief is closely related to anxiety. When your mind dwells on worst-case scenarios, your goal should be to intentionally balance them with thoughts about best-case scenarios. Bring yourself into the present, let go of what you can't control, and stock up on compassion.

✓ There is a sixth stage of grief: meaning. In this dark time, people are finding meaning through connection and are realizing they are not as remote from each other as they thought.

*Adapted from "That Discomfort You're Feeling Is Grief" on hbr.org, March 23, 2020 (product #H05HVE).*

# Section 4

# SEEING BEYOND THE CRISIS

# ENSURE THAT YOUR CUSTOMER RELATIONSHIPS OUTLAST CORONAVIRUS

by Ted Waldron and James Wetherbe

The Covid-19 pandemic has forced businesses to maintain and build relationships with consumers when their world has been upended. Businesses are now facing tension between generating sales during a period of extreme economic hardship and respecting the threats to life and livelihood that have altered consumer priorities and preferences.

This tension is very real, particularly for newer ventures or smaller businesses that provide discretionary products and may not have the resources to survive long periods of severely diminished cash flow.

The coronavirus has changed even large, more established companies literally overnight. On March 16, Nordstrom's 380 stores in the United States and Canada bustled with typical Monday activity. Just one day later, all those stores went dark for at least two weeks, as consumers and employees alike were told to stay away due to the risk of spreading the coronavirus. Such is the nature of business in the time of a pandemic.

What can smaller, newer, more vulnerable businesses do to strengthen relationships with consumers when social distancing has minimized or eliminated personal interaction?

Drawing on nearly 70 years of combined experience in business practice, research, and education, we have found that five key strategies help companies weather crises and preserve their bonds with consumers:

*Humanize* your company.

*Educate* about change.

*Assure* stability.

*Revolutionize* offerings.

*Tackle* the future.

These strategies make up what we call the HEART framework of sustained crisis communication. It provides guidelines on what to say—and what not to say—to consumers during ongoing crises. It emphasizes making current and potential customers aware of your company's plan for supporting them and providing new value that they might require. We'll illustrate the components of the framework by drawing on examples ranging from a big financial services firm (Fidelity Investments) to an auto garage (one that we frequent in New Mexico).

## Humanize Your Company

Let consumers know that your company understands the dire social circumstances at play and cares about more than simply reaping profit during this difficult time. Empathize with those affected by Covid-19, and spell out the steps you are taking to help customers, employees, and other stakeholders. Your company's social media sites and customer mailing lists are ideal vehicles for doing this.

For example, many restaurants are redeploying staff to deliver food, rather than laying them off. Sugarfish, a sushi restaurant chain in New York City and Los Angeles, told customers it would reassign all front-of-house employees to make personalized deliveries rather than outsourcing to delivery services. Having familiar servers deliver familiar menu items helps patrons feel reassured and comforted, and reinforces loyalty by reminding them of what they loved about the restaurant before the crisis.

In another example, financial institutions are forgiving upcoming payments. That's a great way to promote trust and goodwill. As a virus prevention precaution that has a useful element of promotion, Fidelity is asking customers to keep the Fidelity-branded pen used for transactions. The pen will remind customers that Fidelity cared about both their physical and financial health during a time of crisis, reinforcing loyalty after the crisis lifts.

In communicating to your customer about what you can offer them, keep your message brief and classy. Although consumers certainly care about the "softer side" of your business, don't overplay it. Ultimately customers will care most about the value you create for them. Also, expressing too much empathy could come across as insincere and blend into the soundscape of other companies saying the same things.

## Educate Consumers About How to Interact with Your Company

Tell them about all changes to your operation, including new hours, facility closures, staff reductions, customer service availability, and ordering options, among others. While you can reference the emergency government regulations that necessitated the changes, it's far better if you are viewed as being proactive and motivated by your customers' best interests.

For instance, companies such as Lululemon and Apple knew that forced store closings were coming, and they shuttered their stores before the government ordered it. They reached out to their customer list to encourage online shopping, emphasizing their convenient return policies and responsive call services that could help customers with problems and questions.

## Assure Consumers That the Company's Values Will Continue

Elaborate how, despite the upheaval in your operations, you will continue to provide the things they have come to know and love—the defining reasons they patronize your business instead of others. If consumers value the impeccable quality of your wares or the thoughtful nature of your customer service, tell them how you will maintain those value propositions.

For instance, Yoga8, a yoga studio in Waco, Texas, that prides itself on detailed, hands-on instruction, announced the conversion of its courses to online interactive and recorded meetings. Employees of Hans Wittler's Automotive Service in Albuquerque, New Mexico, which prides itself on convenience and safety, now pick up vehicles for repair at customers' homes and return them later.

Elaborating these points of assurance is important in reminding consumers that your company's value proposition—your worth to them—transcends the obstacles imposed by this crisis.

## Revolutionize What Consumers Value About Your Business

Sun Tzu, who penned *The Art of War*, recognized that chaos presents opportunity for innovation. This sentiment has reverberated through the ages. Beyond assuring customers that your company's existing value propositions will remain the same, tell them what innovations

have arisen from dealing with the ongoing pandemic—
after all, necessity is the mother of invention.

Tell your existing customers how you are serving them
in new ways. Reach out to potential customers by offering new products or services that solve a novel problem.
For example, the hamburger chain Fuddruckers decided
to address shortages of bread in grocery stores by bak-
ing and selling loaves directly to consumers. Some liquor
companies have decided to produce hand sanitizer from
the alcohol they distill, combating nationwide sanitizer
shortages.

Companies that take these measures, and let consumers know about them, will inject hope into their heart-
ache as they see how companies are developing ways to
make their lives better. Doing so offers the added benefit
of further humanizing a company.

## Tackle the Future

Establish a timeline for when you will reevaluate the
changes to your company's operations. While you must
comply with any government-imposed limits, do more if
you can afford to. Show customers that, for their benefit,
you are willing to go beyond what you need to do, particularly if your company can handle the financial burden.

Your company can demonstrate going "above and beyond" in various ways, all of which point to silver linings in the pandemic experience. Make it evident that your company is well positioned to maintain its revised business model until things return to normal, signaling that it is weathering the storm. Moreover, highlight what your company has learned from the pandemic experience, as well as how those learnings might improve the way your company operates after the pandemic ends. That is, signal that your company will come out stronger on the other side of the storm. The temporary improvements that satisfy customers now may become permanent enhancements to your company's business model in the future. This will inspire confidence.

The key here is to signal that your company is taking ownership of the situation as much as possible, rather than allowing the situation to take ownership of your company and its valued customers.

With the right customer-centric attitude and an awareness of what people need right now, companies can emerge from this crisis having strengthened their relationships with customers. Give consumers your HEART during this difficult time. It will cultivate long-lasting goodwill with past customers and help ensure that they stay with you in the future.

**TAKEAWAYS**

What can businesses do to preserve relationships with their customers at a time when uncertainty abounds and social distancing has forced storefronts to close? Use the HEART framework to communicate with your customers.

✓ *Humanize* your company. Let consumers know that your business cares about more than simply reaping profit during this difficult time.

✓ *Educate* about change. Tell them about all the changes to your operation, including new hours, closures, staff reductions, and ordering options, among others.

✓ *Assure* stability. Communicate how you will continue to provide the things your customers have come to know and love—the defining reasons they patronize your business instead of others.

✓ *Revolutionize* offerings. Tell them how you are serving them in new ways. Reach out to potential customers with offerings that solve a new problem.

✓  *Tackle* the future. Establish a timeline for when you will reevaluate the changes to your company's operations.

*Adapted from "Ensure That Your Customer Relationships Outlast Coronavirus" on hbr.org, April 1, 2020 (product #H05IQ8).*

# 12

# UNDERSTANDING THE ECONOMIC SHOCK OF CORONAVIRUS

by Philipp Carlsson-Szlezak, Martin Reeves, and Paul Swartz

A s the coronavirus continues its march around the world, governments have turned to proven public health measures, such as social distancing, to physically disrupt the contagion. Yet doing so has severed the flow of goods and people, has stalled economies, and is in the process of delivering a global recession. Economic contagion has spread as fast as the disease itself.

This didn't look plausible even in early March. As the virus began to spread, politicians, policy makers, and markets, informed by the pattern of historical outbreaks, looked on while the early (and thus more effective and less costly) window for social distancing closed. Now, much farther along the disease trajectory, the economic costs are much higher, and predicting the path ahead has become nearly impossible, as multiple dimensions of the crisis are unprecedented and unknowable.

In this uncharted territory, naming a global recession adds little clarity beyond setting the expectation of negative growth. Pressing questions include what path the shock and recovery will take, whether economies will be able to return to their preshock output levels and growth rates, and whether there will be any structural legacy from the coronavirus crisis.

## Darker Outlook, Less Visibility

The window for social distancing—the only known approach to effectively addressing the disease—is short. In Hubei province it was missed, but the rest of China made sure not to miss it. In Italy the window was missed, and then the rest of Europe missed it too. In the United States, which was constrained by insufficient testing, the early window was also missed. As the disease proliferates, social-distancing measures will have to be enacted more broadly and for longer to achieve the same effect, choking economic activity in the process.

Another wave of infections remains a real possibility, meaning even countries that acted relatively quickly are still at risk every time they nudge their economies back to work. Indeed, we have seen resurgence of the virus in Singapore and Hong Kong. In that sense, only history will tell if their early and aggressive responses paid off.

At present, the economic outlook for late actors looks bleak, having caught politicians, policy makers, and financial markets off guard. What happened in March was not part of the risk calculation. Forecasts won't help much here. For example, consensus estimates for initial unemployment claims in the United States were around 1.6 million for the week ending March 27, but the figure came in at 3.28 million—a historically unprecedented figure at the time, about five times greater than the largest weekly increase during the global financial crisis. Notoriously unreliable at the best of times, forecasts look especially dubious now, as there are simply too many unknowable aspects:

- The virus's properties are not fully understood and could change.

- The role of asymptomatic patients is still imperfectly understood.

- The true rates of infection and immunity are therefore uncertain, especially where testing is limited.

- Policy responses will be uneven and often delayed, and there will be missteps.

- The reactions of firms and households are uncertain.

Perhaps the only certainty is that any attempt at a definitive forecast will fail. However, we think examining various scenarios still adds value in this environment of limited visibility.

## Examining the Shape of the Shock

The concept of a recession is binary and blunt. All it says is that expectations have flipped from positive to negative growth, at least for two consecutive quarters.

We think the bigger-scenario question revolves around the shape of the shock—what we call "shock geometry"—and its structural legacy. What drives the economic impact path of a shock, and where does Covid-19 fit in?

To illustrate, consider how the same shock—the global financial crisis—led to recessions with vastly different progressions and recoveries in three sample countries (see figure 12-1).

FIGURE 12-1

## Economic shock: Three examples

*The concept of a recession is binary and blunt. The bigger-scenario question revolves around the shape of the shock and its structural legacy. To illustrate, consider how the 2008 global financial crisis delivered recessions in three sample countries, yet followed vastly different shapes in terms of shock progression and recovery.*

**V-shaped (Canada)**

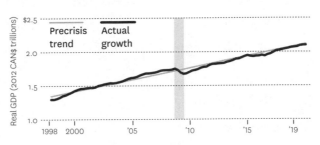

**U-shaped (United States)**

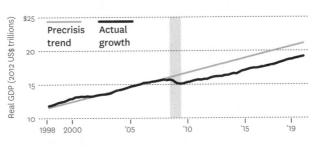

**L-shaped (Greece)**

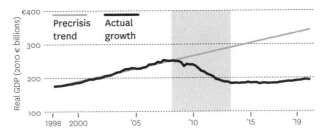

*Sources:* Statistics Canada, NBER, BEA, Hellenic Statistical Authority, BCG Center for Macroeconomics analysis

- **V-shape.** In 2008, Canada avoided a banking crisis:
  Credit continued to flow, and capital formation
  was not significantly disrupted. Avoiding a deeper
  collapse helped keep labor in place and prevented
  skill atrophy. GDP dropped but substantially
  climbed back to its precrisis path. This is typical of
  a classic V-shaped shock, where output is displaced
  but growth eventually rebounds to its old path.

- **U-shape.** The United States had a markedly different
  path. Growth dropped precipitously and never re-
  bounded to its precrisis path. Note that the growth
  *rate* recovered (the slopes are the same), but the gap
  between the old and new path remains large, rep-
  resenting one-off damage to the economy's supply
  side, and indefinitely lost output. This was driven
  by a deep banking crisis that disrupted credit intermediation. As the recession dragged on, it did
  more damage to the labor supply and productivity.
  The shock to the U.S. economy in 2008 followed a
  classic U-shape—a much more costly version than
  Canada's V-shape.

- **L-shape.** Greece is the third example and followed
  by far the worst shape—not only has the country
  never recovered its prior output path, but its growth
  rate has declined. The distance between the old and

new path is widening, with lost output continuously growing. This means the crisis has left lasting structural damage to the economy's supply side. Capital inputs, labor inputs, and productivity are repeatedly damaged. Greece can be seen as an example of an L-shape, by far the most pernicious.

So what drives "shock geometry" as shown above? The key determinant is the shock's ability to damage an economy's supply side and, more specifically, capital formation. When credit intermediation is disrupted and the capital stock doesn't grow, recovery is slow, workers exit the workforce, skills are lost, productivity goes down. The shock becomes structural.

V, U, and L shocks can come in different intensities. A V-shaped path may be shallow or deep. A U-shape may come with a deep drop to a new growth path or a small one.

Where does the coronavirus shock fit in so far? The intensity of the shock will be determined by the underlying virus properties, policy responses, and consumer and corporate behavior in the face of adversity. But the shape of the shock is determined by the virus's capacity to damage economies' supply side, particularly capital formation. At this point, both a deep V-shape and a U-shape are plausible. The battle ahead is to prevent a clear U trajectory.

## Understand the Damage Mechanisms

Keeping the above geometries in mind, this leads to two questions about the Covid-19 shock:

- What is the mechanism for damage to the supply side?

- What is the policy response to prevent such damage?

Classically, financial crises cripple an economy's supply side. There is a long history of such crises, and policy makers have learned much about dealing with them. But the coronavirus extends problems in liquidity and capital to the real economy—and does so at unprecedented scale. As though the twin risks of financial and real liquidity shocks were not enough, they are also interrelated, raising the stakes.

Let's look in more detail at the two paths through which Covid-19 could deliver structural damage in a U-shaped scenario (see figure 12-2):

- **Financial system risks.** The unprecedented Covid-19 shock has already generated stress in capital markets, triggering a forceful response from central banks. If liquidity problems persist and real

FIGURE 12-2

## Two economic supply-side threats from Covid-19

*The Covid-19 shock uniquely raises liquidity and capital risks in both the financial system and the real economy simultaneously.*

|  | Financial system shock | Real economy "freeze" |
|---|---|---|
| Liquidity problems | Liquidity problems hamper credit intermediation and investment | Healthy households and companies face severe cash-flow problems, hampering investment |
| Capital problems | Capital problems shut credit channel, damaging capital formation and ultimately growth | Damaged household and company balance sheets cripple investment and ultimately growth |

*Source:* BCG Center for Macroeconomics analysis

economy problems lead to write-downs, capital problems can arise. While from a policy perspective we may know the solutions, bailouts and recapitalization of banks are politically controversial. In the case of a financial crisis, capital formation would take a huge hit, driving a prolonged slump with damage to labor and productivity as well.

- **Extended real economy "freeze."** The truly unprecedented possibility. Months of social distancing could disrupt capital formation and ultimately labor participation and productivity growth. Unlike financial crises, an extended freeze of this magnitude that damages the supply side would be new territory for policy makers.

The financial and real economy risks are interrelated in two ways: First, a prolonged Covid-19 crisis could drive up the number of real economy bankruptcies, which makes it even harder for the financial system to manage. Meanwhile, a financial crisis would starve the real economy of credit.

It is fair to say the risk profile of the Covid-19 crisis is particularly threatening. While there is a policy playbook for dealing with financial crises, no such thing exists for a large-scale real economy freeze. There is no off-the-shelf cure for liquidity problems of entire real economies.

## Innovating Out of the Shock

It is important to recognize that none of the shock scenarios outlined above will be inevitable, linear, or uniform across geographies. Countries will have considerably different experiences for two reasons: the structural resilience of economies to absorb such shocks (call it destiny) and the capacity of medical researchers and policy makers to respond in new ways to an unprecedented challenge (call it innovation). Can they create novel interventions, at unprecedented speed, that will break the intractable and unattractive trade-off between lost lives and economic misery?

**On the medical side:** It's clear that a vaccine would reduce the need for social distancing and thus relax the policy's chokehold on the global economy. But timelines are likely long, and so the focus may well have to be on incremental innovation within the confines of existing solutions.

Examples of such innovation may be found across the entire medical spectrum. On the therapeutic end, existing treatments may prove effective in fighting the disease. Several dozen existing treatments are currently being evaluated. On the other end of the spectrum, organizational innovation will be needed to free up capacity to meet the demand for resources, such as the optimal mobilization of medical professionals, repurposing of spaces for treatment, and changes to triaging medical care to prioritize the Covid-19 crisis.

**On the economic side:** In the United States, politicians have passed a $2 trillion stimulus package to soften the blow of the coronavirus crisis. But policy innovation also will have to occur. For example, central banks operate so-called discount windows that provide unlimited short-term finance to ensure that liquidity problems don't break the banking system. What is needed now, today, is a "real economy discount window" that can also deliver unlimited liquidity to sound households and firms.

The emerging policy landscape includes many worthwhile ideas. Among them: zero-interest "bridge loans" offered to households and firms for the duration of the crisis and with a generous repayment period; a moratorium on mortgage payments for residential and commercial borrowers; using bank regulators to lean on banks to provide finance and to rework terms on existing loans. Such policy innovations could meaningfully soften the virus's impact on economies' supply side. Yet they also need agile and efficient execution.

We think there is a chance for innovation to prevent a full-blown U-shape, keeping the shock's path closer to a deep V-shape than would otherwise be possible. But the battle is under way, and without innovation the odds are not in favor of the less damaging V-shaped scenario.

TAKEAWAYS

Social distancing to mitigate coronavirus has severed the flow of goods and people, has stalled economies, and is in the process of delivering a global recession. Predicting the path ahead is nearly impossible; multiple dimensions of the crisis are unprecedented and unknowable.

✓ Pressing questions include what path the shock and recovery will take, whether economies will be able to return to their preshock output levels and growth rates, and whether there will be a structural legacy from the crisis.

✓ In looking at scenarios of economic shock, we must confront two questions: *What is the mechanism for damage to the supply side?* and *What is the policy response to prevent such damage?*

✓ The two major paths through which Covid-19 could deliver structural damage are *financial system risks* and *extended real economy "freeze."*

✓ No single shock scenario will be inevitable, linear, or uniform across geographies. Countries will have different experiences based on the structural resilience of their economies and the ways that their medical experts and policy makers respond in new ways to these challenges.

*Adapted from "Understanding the Economic Shock of Coronavirus" on hbr.org, March 27, 2020 (product #H05INL).*

# 13

# WHAT WILL U.S. LABOR PROTECTIONS LOOK LIKE AFTER CORONAVIRUS?

by Megan Tobias Neely

A s I was writing the draft of this article, I was checking my symptoms and awaiting the results of a test
I underwent for Covid-19. This virus has upended
my life, as it has for every last one of us, no matter where
we fall on the socioeconomic scale.

But the consequences fall more heavily on those at the
bottom end of the wage distribution. That includes those

risking their health as they sell us groceries, check our vitals, and sanitize our hospitals. Easily lost amid the chaos, however, is how this crisis may be an opportunity to improve employee protections—and not temporarily but permanently.

During bull markets, employers and policy makers often paint the hardships befalling low-wage workers as stemming from those workers' personal failures. But when markets crash, we learn how the workers' troubles were indicative of persistent, system-wide weaknesses.

As Warren Buffett wrote of the insurance failures exposed by 1993's Hurricane Andrew, "It's only when the tide goes out that you learn who's been swimming naked." Pundits cite Buffett to refer to firms that appear healthy during bull markets, only to get eaten alive during downturns. Now, however, the markets are exposing a new group of skinny-dippers: a government and an economic system that fail workers, and employers who haven't filled or can't fill this gap in public policy.

In response to the novel coronavirus, the stock market has been mostly in a free fall since late February. The low-wage service sector is facing widespread layoffs. And the tumbling markets have uncovered other deep inequalities among workers, who fall into two groups: those with access to employment protections like affordable health care, remote work accommodations, paid time off, and job security—and those without.

This second group, which includes the working class, often lack health care or face high out-of-pocket expenses. There are nearly 24 million uninsured working-age adults in the United States. Those with only a high school diploma or who did not complete high school are the least likely to be insured. Moreover, racial and ethnic minority groups face significant barriers to "good jobs." They form 60% of the uninsured population but only 40% of the total population.

A quarter of all U.S. workers have no access to paid sick leave. Work-from-home options are slim, but many can't afford not to work. Among workers at the bottom 10th of the earnings distribution, only 31% have paid sick leave. For comparison, 94% of the top 10% of earners have paid sick leave.

While many professionals enjoy protections that can help them ride out the pandemic with their livelihoods and family's health intact, workers in the low-wage service sector have few options or resources to stay home to care for themselves, let alone their loved ones. And that burden to provide care largely falls on women. The workers lacking health care and paid sick leave are also the most vulnerable to layoffs and lost hours. The fate of service workers in travel and food services indicate what's to come. Similarly, gig economy workers, migrant laborers, and those in the informal economy are particularly vulnerable.

How did we get here? Since the late 1970s, executives have prioritized boosting dividends for shareholders over protecting their employees, whose work has been outsourced, digitized, and downsized. In our book, *Divested: Inequality in the Age of Finance*, Ken-Hou Lin and I show how this shift in corporate governance undermined workers' bargaining power. Although insurance coverage increased following the Affordable Care Act, overall working conditions, protections, and pay have diminished.

A more robust safety net would help to mitigate the consequences for workers today as it shores up the economy against future downturns. For years, U.S. policy makers have considered universal health care impractical because of its large scope and high startup costs. But as new unemployment claims surge to historical levels and Americans face the medical precarity of a pandemic, this crisis has laid bare the underlying problem of linking health care to employment.

Sick leave and universal health care would ease the stressors workers face and ensure that the sick have time to recover, making them more productive when they return to work. Without the costs of insuring workers, employers could pay more. An income boost would generate more spending and stimulate the economy.

Broader protections would also support the self-employed, contract workers, and prospective entrepreneurs. The United States has lower rates of self-employment (6.3%) than countries with universal health care (e.g., Spain has 16%), and a lower share of employment at small businesses than any OECD member country except Russia. Reducing the reliance on big businesses would free workers to find jobs that better fit their skills, creating a more nimble and innovative economy.

The current moment provides an opportunity to make lasting changes to the status quo and improve conditions for all workers. As sociologists have theorized, crises and crashes expose cracks in the systems upholding inequality. And history provides a clue for how crises can provide opportunities to transform society in ways that reduce inequality. After the Great Crash of 1929, unemployment spiked, reaching 25% by 1933. In less than three years, Franklin D. Roosevelt's New Deal reduced unemployment to 9%. The New Deal achieved this feat through a vast and broad range of public works and conservation projects.

The New Deal transformed American society—from erecting iconic buildings and statues, to saving the whooping crane, to developing the rural United States, to planting a billion trees. New Deal workers built and renovated 2,500 hospitals, 45,000 schools, and 700,000 miles of roads. The New Deal hired 60% of the unemployed, including 50,000 teachers and 3,000 writers and artists, such as Jackson Pollock and Willem de Kooning. The New Deal modernized, preserved, and employed the country, while reducing inequality between the haves and have-nots.

Facing a similar economic threat in the wake of the pandemic, we have a comparable once-in-a-century opportunity to make lasting changes that address the pressing problems of today, from inequality to climate change.

In today's crisis, we could follow the "trickle-down" approach to stimulus that was adopted during the 2008 financial crisis: providing stimulus to the banks, corporations, and their investors combined with tax cuts and temporary wage support as a short-term Band-Aid for immiserated workers. But Lin and I find that this approach left many workers flailing and worsened inequality, because the banks deposited, rather than invested, the stimulus funding, and corporations borrowed the money to buy back their stocks, enriching top executives and shareholders.

In late March, the president signed into law a sweeping $2 trillion plan that combines money for states, loans for distressed businesses, and tax relief, paid leave, unemployment benefits, and cash for most citizens. But this plan only gives workers *temporary* benefits. Although the bill includes stricter oversight than the 2008 stimulus package and restricts stock buybacks, it is unlikely to reduce inequality unless it addresses the structural conditions making some workers more vulnerable.

While a New Deal approach may be infeasible amid a contagious virus, we can and should enact *permanent* policies protecting *all* workers. Sick leave and health care should be universal rights. We could adopt a "flexicurity" labor policy modeled on the Danish one. The Danes provide both flexibility for employers to hire and fire workers as needed and security for workers through generous benefits and retraining opportunities during unemployment.

Meanwhile, in my household, after 2.5 weeks of symptoms—from a dry cough to a tight chest to a low fever—my test results came back negative. Thanks to the health care and insurance provided by my employer, I will continue to do the work I care about.

While I am on the mend, the workers who sell our groceries, serve us food, clean our workplaces, and drive us to the doctor also need to take care. In this pandemic, they are risking their health and lives. And they deserve the same level of care as the people they serve: access to both preventative medicine and comprehensive treatment, and time to take a break, recover, and care for their loved ones. The coronavirus is our chance to extend these protections during times of crisis and far into the future.

TAKEAWAYS

The consequences of the Covid-19 pandemic fall more heavily on lower-wage workers, including those risking their health as they sell us groceries, check our vitals, and sanitize our hospitals.

✓ During bull markets, employers and policy makers often paint the hardships befalling low-wage workers as stemming from those workers' personal failures. But when markets crash, we learn how the workers' troubles were indicative of persistent, system-wide weaknesses.

✓ The U.S. government response to the 2008 financial crisis was a "trickle-down" approach: stimulus to banks, corporations, and their investors combined with tax cuts and temporary wage support as a short-term Band-Aid for immiserated workers that left many workers flailing and worsened inequality.

✓ This crisis is an opportunity to improve employee protections permanently. Sick leave and health care should be universal rights, and a "flexicurity" labor policy could provide both flexibility for employers to hire and fire workers as needed and security for workers through generous benefits and retraining opportunities during unemployment.

*Adapted from "What Will U.S. Labor Protections Look Like After Coronavirus?" on hbr.org, April 2, 2020 (product #H05IQ0).*

14

# WE NEED IMAGINATION NOW MORE THAN EVER

by Martin Reeves and Jack Fuller

T he idea of "crisis management" requires no explanation right now. Something unexpected and significant happens, and our first instincts are to defend
against—and later to understand and manage—the dis-
turbance to the status quo. The crisis is an unpredictable
enemy to be tamed for the purpose of restoring normality.

But we may not be able to return to our familiar precrisis reality. Pandemics, wars, and other social crises often
create new attitudes, needs, and behaviors, which need
to be managed. We believe that imagination—the capacity to create, evolve, and exploit mental models of things

or situations that don't yet exist—is the crucial factor in seizing and creating new opportunities, and finding new paths to growth.

Imagination is also one of the hardest things to keep alive under pressure. Companies that are able to do so can reap significant value. In recessions and downturns, 14% of companies outperform both historically and competitively, because they invest in new growth areas.[1] For example, Apple released its first iPod in 2001—the same year the U.S. economy experienced a recession that contributed to a 33% drop in the company's total revenue. Still, Apple saw the iPod's ability to transform its product portfolio: It increased R&D spending by double digits. The launch of the iTunes Store (2003) and new iPod models (2004) sparked an era of high growth.

With imagination, we can do better than merely *adapting* to a new environment—we can thrive by *shaping* it. To do this, we need to strategize across multiple timescales, each requiring a different style of thinking. In the current Covid-19 crisis, for example:

- The initial emphasis is on rapid *reaction* and defense.

- Then the focus shifts to constructing and implementing plans to endure the likely economic *recession* to follow.

- As the recession abates, the focus shifts to *rebound*—making adjustments to portfolios and channels as we seek to exploit recovering demand.

- Over time the situation becomes more malleable, and imaginative companies shift their focus to *reinventing*—seeking opportunity in adversity by applying more creative approaches to strategy.

In other words, renewal and adaptive strategies give way to classical planning-based strategies and then to visionary and shaping strategies, which require imagination.

We recently surveyed more than 250 multinational companies to understand the measures they were taking to manage the Covid-19 epidemic (see figure 14-1). While most companies are enacting a rich portfolio of reactive measures, only a minority are yet at the stage where they're identifying and shaping strategic opportunities.

We have written elsewhere about what the post-Covid reality will probably look like and how to discriminate between temporary and enduring shifts in demand.[2] But how can companies avoid having imagination become the first casualty of the crisis? Phrased another way, how can you develop your organization's capacity for imagination? Based on our research for a new book on the imaginative corporation, we share seven imperatives.

FIGURE 14-1

# Which measures are companies taking in response to Covid-19?

*BCG surveyed more than 250 multinational companies on the actions they were taking in response to the Covid-19 pandemic. While most firms are enacting a rich portfolio of defensive measures, only a minority are identifying and shaping strategic opportunities.*

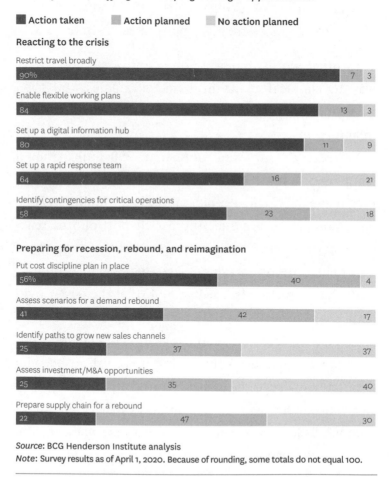

■ Action taken    ■ Action planned    ■ No action planned

**Reacting to the crisis**

Restrict travel broadly
90% | 7 | 3

Enable flexible working plans
84 | 13 | 3

Set up a digital information hub
80 | 11 | 9

Set up a rapid response team
64 | 16 | 21

Identify contingencies for critical operations
58 | 23 | 18

**Preparing for recession, rebound, and reimagination**

Put cost discipline plan in place
56% | 40 | 4

Assess scenarios for a demand rebound
41 | 42 | 17

Identify paths to grow new sales channels
25 | 37 | 37

Assess investment/M&A opportunities
25 | 35 | 40

Prepare supply chain for a rebound
22 | 47 | 30

*Source*: BCG Henderson Institute analysis
*Note*: Survey results as of April 1, 2020. Because of rounding, some totals do not equal 100.

# 1. Carve Out Time for Reflection

Crises place heavy demands on leaders and managers, and it is easy to lose the already slim time we might have for reflection. But we won't see the big picture, let alone a shapeable picture of the future, unless we stand back and reflect.

Most of the time in business we operate with our instinctual "fight-or-flight" nervous system that evolved to help us in high-pressure situations, like running from a predator. This system narrows our focus. But lesser known is the parasympathetic, or "rest-and-digest" system, which evolved to manage mental and bodily operations when we are relaxed. We can imagine our ancestors in hunter-gatherer days engaged in the mental intensity of the hunt, followed by time back at home, reflecting on the day's stories, perhaps envisioning how to hunt better.

We need to create the equivalent rhythm of action and reflection in business as we navigate this crisis. Ways to switch off fight-or-flight mode and support reflection include:

- Taking a few deep in-breaths and longer out-breaths

- Taking time over a meal to rest, digest, and reflect

- Listening to or playing music

- Going for a walk without your phone

## 2. Ask Active, Open Questions

In a crisis, we likely won't have immediate answers, and we therefore need to employ good questions. The most natural questions in a crisis tend to be *passive*, for example, "What will happen to us?" However, the possibility of shaping events to our advantage only arises if we ask *active* questions, such as "How can we create new options?"

Creativity involves reaching beyond precedents and known alternatives to ask questions that prompt the exploration of fresh ideas and approaches. Some good questions to ask in the Covid-19 crisis might include:

- Which needs or products are taking center stage?

- What customer needs exist for which there is no current solution?

- What are we *not* doing for our customers?

- If we were starting over now, what company and offering would we build?

- Why are today's loyal customers still doing business with us?

# 3. Allow Yourself to Be Playful

Crises require goal-driven and serious responses. However, in times of stress, we tend to overlook the important human capacity of play to temporarily forget about goals and improvise. Biologically, play can be characterized as derisked, accelerated learning. For example, juvenile animals' mock fighting is highly effective preparation for real combat.

In unprecedented, rapidly changing situations, play is a critical capability. As well as providing some much-needed stress relief—how many of us are currently working from dawn to dusk?—play can end up being, counterintuitively, very productive. We can make interesting new connections between ideas when we allow ourselves to loosen up from our regular, goal-driven, laser-focused, instrumental approach.

"Creativity is the rearrangement of existing knowledge into new, useful combinations," Jorgen Vig Knudstorp, chairman of the LEGO Brand Group, told us. "Just like playing with LEGO Bricks, this can lead you to valuable innovations—like the Google search engine or the Airbnb business model."

Sometimes nothing immediately useful will come of play, but playing at least allows us to practice imagining, improvising, and being open to inspiration—all important skills when navigating the unknown.

## 4. Set Up a System for Sharing Ideas

Someone, somewhere in your organization is likely being forced by circumstances to experiment with new ways of doing things. The imaginative corporation picks up, codifies, and scales these innovations.

Imagination doesn't just happen on an individual level. Ideas evolve and spread by being able to skip between minds. Companies need to facilitate collective imagination. The key to this is allowing new ideas to be shared while they are still in development: creating forums for people to communicate in a casual way, without hierarchy, reports, permissions, or financial justifications.

Conversely, the way to kill imagination and the spread of ideas is to construct noncommunicating functional silos and to induce fear of not meeting the bar for "sensible" suggestions. In the name of "practicality" or "common sense," many ideas are rejected without being explored. But it is hard to distinguish ideas with no eventual merit from those which are merely unfamiliar, undeveloped, counterintuitive, or countercultural. In a situation where there are no easy solutions, we need to *open up* rather than constrict the funnel for new ideas.

Every corporation had entrepreneurial beginnings. But successful corporations that have honed a stable, profitable, business recipe forget the messy, imaginative origins of the ideas upon which they were founded. Now is not the time for only executing a practiced recipe. We are facing a historic discontinuity, requiring entrepreneurialism and creativity.

## 5. Seek Out the Anomalous and Unexpected

Imagination is triggered by surprising inputs. Our pattern-seeking minds adapt our mental models when we see something that does not fit. And when we adapt our mental models, we entertain different strategies and courses of action.

To solve tough new problems, look externally. Examine accidents, anomalies, and particulars, and ask, "What doesn't fit here?" Digging into what we find will prompt reframing, rethinking, and the discovery of new possibilities.

In the current situation, we might ask, for example: Why have some countries like Japan, China, and South Korea been able to break away from an exponential infection pattern? Or why are some cities suffering more than others? Or why have apparently similar strategies given different results in different places? Or what stopped us from being prepared for this crisis in spite of MERS, SARS, Ebola, and other ominous precedents?

# 6. Encourage Experimentation

Although a crisis stretches our resources, it is important to encourage experiments—even if only on a shoestring budget. Natural systems are most resilient when they are diverse, and that diversity comes from trying new ways of doing new things. Our ideas only become useful if they are tested in the real world, often generating unexpected outcomes and stimulating further thinking and new ideas.

For example, Ole Kirk Christiansen, the founder of the LEGO Brand, originally made homes and household products, such as wooden ladders and ironing boards, until the Great Depression of the 1930s forced him to experiment, and he tried building toys. This turned out to be a successful move at a time when consumers were holding back from building homes. After examining the international toy market, which was largely derived from wood, Christiansen was driven to experiment again by introducing toys made of a new, disruptive material—plastic. He reinvested a full year's profits into new machinery and tools, at first making traditional toys, then creating building blocks. By 1958, these had evolved into today's well-known "binding" LEGO Bricks. Soon after, the company abandoned all wooden and other toys to double down on the LEGO Brick Toy Building System).

# 7. Stay Hopeful

Imagination feeds off the aspirations and aggravations that propel us to seek a better reality. When we lose hope and adopt a passive mindset, we cease to believe that we can meet our ideals or fix our problems. In statistics, Bayesian learning involves taking a belief about a statistical distribution (a "prior") and updating it in the light of each new piece of information obtained. The outcome of the entire process can be determined by the initial belief. Pessimism can become a self-fulfilling prophesy.

As a leader, ask yourself whether you are giving people grounds for hope, imagination, and innovation, or whether you are using pessimistic or fatalistic language, which could create a downward spiral in organizational creativity. Dealing with real risks involves taking imaginative risks, which requires hope.

"Never in our lifetimes has the power of imagination been more important in defining our immediate future," Jim Loree, CEO of Stanley Black & Decker, told us. "Leaders need to seize the opportunity to inspire and harness the imagination of their organizations during this challenging time."

All crises contain the seeds of opportunity. Many businesses, struggling now, will likely find a second life during and after the crisis, if they can keep alive and harness their imaginations. Imagination may seem like a frivolous luxury in a crisis, but it is actually a necessity for building future success.

## TAKEAWAYS

Many businesses, struggling now, will find a second life during and after the pandemic. Cultivating imagination now may seem like a luxury, but it is actually a necessity for building future success.

- ✓ **Carve out time for reflection.** Switch from "fight-or-flight" mode to "rest-and-reflect" mode.

- ✓ **Ask active, open questions.** Reach beyond precedents and known alternatives to explore fresh ideas.

- ✓ **Allow yourself to be playful.** Make interesting, new connections between ideas by letting go of the regular goal-driven approach.

- ✓ **Set up a system for sharing ideas.** Facilitate *collective* imagination. Ideas are able to evolve and spread by being able to skip between minds.

- ✓ **Seek out the anomalous and unexpected.** Look externally to solve tough new problems. Imagination is triggered by surprising inputs.

- ✓ **Encourage experimentation.** Try new ways of doing things. Diversity makes our natural systems more resilient.

- ✓ **Stay hopeful.** Avoid a fatalistic or passive mindset. Imagination feeds off the aspirations and aggravations that propel us to seek a better reality.

## NOTES

1. Martin Reeves, David Rhodes, Christian Ketels, and Kevin Whitaker, "Advantage in Adversity: Winning the Next Downturn," BGC Henderson Institute, January 18, 2019, https://bcghendersoninstitute.com/advantage-in-adversity-winning-the-next-downturn-5853b4425db1.

2. Martin Reeves, Philipp Carlsson-Szlezak, Kevin Whitaker, and Mark Abraham, "Sensing and Shaping the Post-COVID Era," BCG Henderson Institute, March 29, 2020, https://bcghendersoninstitute.com/sensing-and-shaping-the-post-covid-era-c282cd227a4f.

*Adapted from "We Need Imagination Now More Than Ever" on hbr.org, April 10, 2020 (product #H05JYI).*

# About the Contributors

**SCOTT BERINATO** is a senior editor at *Harvard Business Review* and the author of *Good Charts: The HBR Guide to Making Smarter, More Persuasive Data Visualizations* and *Good Charts Workbook: Tips, Tools, and Exercises for Making Better Data Visualizations* (Harvard Business Review Press, 2016, 2019).

**VANESSA K. BOHNS** is an associate professor of Organizational Behavior at the ILR School at Cornell University.

**PHILIPP CARLSSON-SZLEZAK** is a partner and managing director in BCG's New York office and chief economist of BCG.

**ALISA COHN** is an executive coach who specializes in work with *Fortune* 500 companies and prominent startups, including Google, Microsoft, Foursquare, Venmo, and Etsy.

**JACK FULLER** is a project manager at the BCG Henderson Institute. He is a Rhodes Scholar with a background in neuroscience and philosophical theology.

**MICHAEL GERVAIS, PHD,** is a high-performance psychologist whose clients include world-record holders, Olympians, internationally acclaimed artists and musicians, MVPs from every major sport, and *Fortune* 100 CEOs. He is the cofounder of Compete to Create and the host of *Finding Mastery.*

**LAURA M. GIURGE** is a postdoctoral research associate at London Business School and the Barnes Research Fellow at the Wellbeing Research Centre at the University of Oxford. Her research focuses on time, happiness, and the future of work.

**SHOMA CHATTERJEE HAYDEN** coheads ghSMART's leadership development and coaching practice. She focuses on helping CEOs and their teams increase their collective resilience and performance.

**SARAH KALLOCH** is executive director of the Good Jobs Institute, a nonprofit whose mission is to help companies thrive by providing good jobs. Follow her on Twitter @sarahkalloch.

**REBECCA KNIGHT** is a freelance journalist in Boston and a lecturer at Wesleyan University. Her work has been published in the *New York Times*, *USA Today*, and the *Financial Times*.

**NANCY KOEHN** is the James E. Robison Professor of Business Administration at Harvard Business School.

**TSEDAL NEELEY** is the Naylor Fitzhugh Professor of Business Administration in the Organizational Behavior Unit at Harvard Business School and the founder of the consulting firm Global Matters. She is the author of *The Language of Global Success*. Follow her on Twitter @tsedal.

**MEGAN TOBIAS NEELY** is a sociologist and postdoctoral researcher at the VMware Women's Leadership Innovation Lab at Stanford University. She is currently writing a book on the hedge fund industry and coauthored the book *Divested: Inequality in the Age of Finance*.

**CHRIS NICHOLS** is a leadership advisor at ghSMART, where he advises leading corporations and investment firms.

**MARTIN REEVES** is a senior partner and managing director in the San Francisco office of BCG and chairman of the BCG Henderson Institute, BCG's think tank on management and strategy.

**PETER SUSSER** is partner in the global employment and labor law firm Littler Mendelson, based in Washington, DC.

**PAUL SWARTZ** is a director and senior economist in the BCG Henderson Institute, based in BCG's New York office.

**ZEYNEP TON** is a professor of the practice at MIT's Sloan School of Management and cofounder and president of the nonprofit Good Jobs Institute. She is the author of *The Good Jobs Strategy: How the Smartest Companies Invest in Employees to Lower Costs and Boost Profits*. Follow her on Twitter @zeynepton.

**CHRIS TRENDLER** is a partner at ghSMART, where he serves leaders in private-equity-backed and *Fortune* 500 companies on their most critical talent decisions.

**TAHL TYSON** is a partner in the global employment and labor law firm Littler Mendelson. She is a UK solicitor based in Seattle, Washington.

**TED WALDRON** is an associate professor of management at Texas Tech University's Rawls College of Business.

**JAMES WETHERBE** is the Richard Schulze Distinguished Professor at Texas Tech University's Rawls College of Business.

# Index

*Note:* Figures and tables are indicated by *f* and *t*, respectively.

reactive vs. proactive business
strategy, xii, 148–149, 152
real economy freezes, 127*f*,
131–132, 142
recessions and depressions,
economic, 126, 130
Covid-19-related, 123–124,
125, 129, 135
Global Financial Crisis, 125,
126–129, 127*f*, 142
Great Depression, 26, 29,
141–142, 156–157
shock and recovery struc-
tures, 126–129, 127*f*, 134,
148–149, 150*f*
Reeves, Martin, xi–xv,
123–136, 147–159
reflection, xi–xii, 151–152
reliability, in leadership, 7–8
remote work
avoiding burnout, 93–100
business culture, 43–44, 50, 51
disease transmission and,
65, 66
emotional/personality as-
pects, 41, 49, 83, 87–88
questions and answers, 39–51
technological tools, 40–41,
42, 43, 45–48
transitions and logistics,
40–43, 48–50
respect for employees,
76–78, 140

rest-and-digest system,
151–152
restaurants, 116, 119
retailers
"can't-close," and safety,
71–79
closures, 114, 117
return-to-work policies, 17
Roosevelt, Eleanor, 29
Roosevelt, Franklin D., 26, 29,
141–142
routine, remote work, 41

safety. *See* employee and
company safety
salaries. *See* employee
compensation
sales workforce
maintaining customer
relationships, 113–114
virtual transitions and
processes, 48
sanitization, 16, 72, 73,
76, 119
schedules. *See* work hours and
schedules
"second wave" infections, 125
self-care
importance, and leaders'
focus, 8, 32–34, 60, 61,
84–90
methods, 33, 61, 84–88, 90